Critical Guides to French Texts

EDITED BY ROGER LITTLE, WOLFGANG VAN EMDEN, DAVID WILLIAMS

ALAIN-FOURNIER

Le Grand Meaulnes

Robert Gibson

Professor of French,
University of Kent at Canterbury

Grant & Cutler Ltd
1986

© Grant & Cutler Ltd
1986
ISBN 0 7293 0237 7

I.S.B.N. 84-599-1042-3

DEPÓSITO LEGAL: V. 1.928 - 1985

Printed in Spain by
Artes Gráficas Soler, S.A., Valencia
for
GRANT & CUTLER LTD
11 BUCKINGHAM STREET, LONDON W.C.2

Contents

References

References to the text of *Le Grand Meaulnes* given by figures in parentheses are to the edition by Robert Gibson (London, Harrap, 1968). This contains a full life of the author, a detailed study of the genesis of the novel and a selection of extracts from early and suppressed versions of the final work.

References to other works listed in the Bibliographical Note give the number of the work in italics, followed by the page number, thus: *7*, p.145.

I refer throughout to the author of *Le Grand Meaulnes* as 'Alain-Fournier' though this was, in fact, a pseudonym. He adopted it on the occasion of the publication of his essay 'Le Corps de la femme' in *La Grande Revue* on Christmas Day, 1907. He had originally signed the essay with his real name 'Henri Fournier' but changed this when it was pointed out that there were two people of that name already well known in France, one an admiral, and the other a racing cyclist.

1. The Novelist and his Novel

Although some short poems survive from 1903 when Alain-Fournier was seventeen years old (p.185), the first written expression of his resolve to write dates from March 1905. It occurs in a letter to his schoolteacher parents, voicing his profound regret that officialdom had transferred them from Epineuil-le-Fleuriel, the small village in the south of the Cher *département*, where he spent most of his childhood. He recalled their 'anciennes allées de fraisiers, près du grand, tranquille et silencieux champ du père Martin près du ruisseau, qui s'enfonçaient vers le champ, plein d'ombre, de branches et de mystère... les haies d'aubépine du jardin, pleines d'orties, de menthes, de cerfeuil, d'herbes qui sentaient bon... la vigne vierge du hangar... la petite porte de bois dont le verrou criait et qu'on ouvrait pour voir trois œufs blottis dans la paille'. Because they were grown-ups, their senses dulled by habit and their time and energy devoted to their duties, he was sure that such perceptions had not registered on their consciousness,

> mais nous, nous venions au monde là-dedans, et tout notre cœur, tout notre bonheur, tout ce que nous sentons de doux ou de pénible, nous avons appris à le sentir, à le connaître, dans la cour où, mélancoliques, les jeudis, nous n'entendions que les cris des coqs dans le bourg — et dans la chambre où, par la lucarne, le soleil venait jouer sur mes deux saintes vierges et sur l'oreiller rouge — et dans la classe où entraient avec les branches des pommiers, quand papa faisait 'étude', les soirs, tout le soleil doux et tiède de cinq heures, toute la bonne odeur de la terre bêchée.
>
> Tout cela, voyez-vous, pour moi c'est le monde entier — et il me semble que mon cœur est fait tout entier...
>
> Je voudrais vous écrire des livres et des livres sur tout ce qu'*on* a vu et senti dans ce petit coin de terre où le monde a

tenu pour nous — et sur ce coin de mon cœur où j'aime
encore à le faire tenir. (*8*, pp.54-55)

This adolescent manifesto seems to me to provide proof
positive of its author's literary vocation. It displays the same
degree of emotional control and the same judiciousness in the
choice of precise and suggestive detail that characterize the
rather more celebrated evocation of vanished childhood in
Proust's *Du côté de chez Swann*. It recalls the passage in
Baudelaire's outstanding essay on the painter Constantin Guys,
in which he declares that the mark of the true artist is his ability
to will himself to see the world through the eyes of a child:
'L'enfant voit tout en *nouveauté*; il est toujours *ivre*. Rien ne
ressemble à ce qu'on appelle l'inspiration, que la joie avec
laquelle l'enfant absorbe la forme et la couleur.'[1] He expresses
not so much the comparatively common young person's wish to
become a writer as the relatively rare compulsion to write, the
recognition that his individual perceptions of the world are
unique, irreplaceable and fated to be lost forever unless he can
ensnare them in a web of words.

This same compulsion is strikingly evident in Alain-Fournier's
immediate response to what was to prove the most crucial single
encounter in his life three months later. On Ascension Thursday,
June 1 1905, emerging from an art exhibition in Paris at the
Grand Palais, he saw descending the stone steps just ahead of
him, an elderly lady and a slim, smartly-dressed girl, with
striking blonde hair and a brown cloak loosely draped about her
shoulders. He followed them at a discreet distance along the
Cours-la-Reine and on to a *bateau-mouche* which ferried them
across the Seine. He disembarked when they did and trailed
them until they entered a house in the fashionable boulevard
Saint-Germain. On several occasions thereafter, whenever he
could escape from his boarding-school on the southern outskirts
of Paris, he returned to keep vigil near the girl's front door. On
Whit Sunday, June 11, he was finally able to engage her in conversation. The very first of the few words he was ever to speak to

[1] 'Le Peintre de la vie moderne', in *Curiosités ésthétiques* (*Œuvres complètes*,
Gallimard, Bibliothèque de la Pléiade, 1961), p.1159.

her were 'Vous êtes belle'. He told her he was the son of a country schoolmaster and spoke of his literary ambitions. She revealed that she was an aristocrat, that her father was a high-ranking naval officer based in the south of France and that she was rejoining him there the following day. She told him her name was Yvonne de Quiévrecourt to which he replied 'Le nom que je vous donnais était plus beau'. He could not bring himself to tell her that the name he had already bestowed on her was Mélisande, the flaxen-haired heroine of Debussy's opera to which he and his classmates were passionately devoted. What precisely he went on to say to her has not been recorded. What he never forgot, and went on repeating afterwards in a variety of contexts, were two of her remarks to him: 'A quoi bon? A quoi bon?' whenever he tentatively suggested that they might meet again, and the words which brought their brief encounter to its end: 'Nous sommes deux enfants, nous avons fait une folie. Adieu, ne me suivez pas'. Whereupon, she walked out of his sight and into his dreaming and his writing.

Less remarkable than the fact that he persisted in worshipping her helplessly from afar, long after he discovered that she was married and the mother of two children, is the literary capital which immediately resulted and which continued to accrue. Just as soon as he got back to his boarding-school after first seeing that (still nameless) blonde girl on June 1, he wrenched some pages from an exercise book and, all too evidently writing at great speed, with scant regard for legibility, punctuation or artistic polish, with verbal variants uncancelled and some words unfinished, he tried to record his impressions in all their immediacy. As the *bateau-mouche* chugged its way across the Seine, leaving the Grand Palais in its wake, he looked ahead to where they might eventually arrive:

Il y a du silence sur les berges et comme de la solitude. Le bateau file avec un bruit calme de machine et d'eau dans ce soleil blanc d'après-midi trop calme. Il me semble qu'on va atterrir quelque part qu'elle descendra disparaîtra [*sic*] avec la vieille dame et que la maison est dans un quartier excessivement tranquille — peut-être dans la banlieue, peut-être la campagne, une maison comme une que je connais, avec un espace devant assombri par des marronniers entouré de murs où des roses à quatre pétales jaunes et rouge vif s'effeuillent et sentent un parfum trop chaude et triste. Je songe au pigeonnier dans un coin de cette cour-jardin le plus sombre. Toute la soirée les colombes ou les pigeons roucoulent, elle doit venir lire à côté du pigeonnier à cause de l'ombre, mais pas longtemps, parce que des pigeons qui ont l'air de roucouler chaque minute de l'après-midi chaude et longue sont tristes! Le couloir où les dames qui viennent en visite passent et laissent leurs ombrelles, et la conversation qui va se prolonger jusqu'à 4 ou 5 heures quand les allées ont fraîchi et que les enfants y jouent et que les dames passent pour aller au dîner. (p.xxvii)

This passage is rich in interest and significance. A few weeks later, it was worked up into the most successful of his poems, 'A travers les étés...' (pp.185-88). It is, in essence, the first section he ever wrote of *Le Grand Meaulnes*, several of the words and phrases being transposed directly into the description of the lovers' first meeting at *la fête étrange*. More noteworthy than that, however, is the way in which his impressions of the immediate present so effortlessly modulate into recollections of the distant past: Parisian local colour is entirely absent, the setting is one of the most cherished memories of his lost childhood, the dove-haunted house and garden of Madame Benoist in Epineuil, where, as a special treat, his mother would take him to tea. Although he could never forget that in reality he had met Yvonne in Paris, and that she lived within sight and sound of the sea, in all his subsequent writing, she was invariably to appear against a pastoral background, indissolubly linked with that remote country village which, he had vowed his parents, he would never allow to be forgotten.

From the summer of 1905 onwards, Alain-Fournier's love for Yvonne, his yearning for his rural past and his evolving literary ambitions, all became inextricably intertwined. In January 1907, he wrote to his best friend, Jacques Rivière: 'A moi qui demandais un grand amour impossible et lointain, cet amour est venu' (*7*, p.21), and there seems little doubt that her principal role was to inspire him with lofty thoughts, always with the unspoken promise that she would return his love at the last as just reward for his remaining loyal and pure. Writing to another close friend in 1908, he reasoned that he had fallen in love and continued to love in the way that he did because of the particular circumstances of his country childhood: 'Il faut... pour s'imaginer La Demoiselle, avoir été soi-même quelque enfant paysan; avoir attendu sans fin, les jeudis de juin, derrière la grille d'une cour, près des grandes barrières blanches qui ferment les allées à la lisière des bois du château' (*9*, p.141). His obstinate refusal to give up the hope that he would one day marry her together with the corrosive sense of guilt left by a number of short-lived liaisons both express his conviction that Yvonne's love and his own purity were the surest guarantees of that special childhood vision he deemed to be so vital for his writing.

It took him some time to fashion a literary formula adequate to express that vision in all its particularity. Like many a fledgling author before and since, he needed time to discover who he was, what he really wanted to say and how best to say it; he needed time to digest, then to distance himself from, the emotional upheavals which provided the subject-matter of his writing. His problems were compounded because as well as being an ambitious would-be writer, he was also a voracious and impressionable reader: he kept on hearing echoes of other men's phrases and formulations while he was striving to find his own authentic voice. In 1905 and 1906, he wrote mainly *vers libres* which, though recording authentic memories of his village childhood, read like pastiches of the once popular rural poet Francis Jammes. For much of 1908 and 1909, his preferred formula was to write a number of prose poems connected by the common theme of *l'autre paysage*, that elusive country just beyond the confines of the workaday world which we glimpse occasionally in childhood until we learn adult wisdom and it recedes forever from our view (*30* and *40*). The title of the collection was to have been *Le Pays sans nom*. There is no evidence that Alain-

Fournier was acquainted with Wordsworth's 'Ode on Intimations of Immortality from Recollections of Early Childhood' which so effectively evokes the 'heaven which lies about us in our infancy', but he certainly knew the childhood sections of Rimbaud's *Illuminations* because he declared his intention was to surpass him: 'Mon crédo en art et en littérature: l'enfance. Arriver à la rendre sans aucune puérilité (cf. J-A. Rimbaud), avec sa profondeur qui touche les mystères. Mon livre futur sera peut-être un perpétuel va-et-vient insensible du rêve à la réalité; "rêve" entendu comme l'immense et imprécise vie enfantine planant au-dessus de l'autre et sans cesse mise en rumeur par les échos de l'autre' (6, p.323). In the event, he wrote only a handful of prose poems on this theme but, consistent with his policy of exploiting any fragment of his early writing which might serve a turn, he incorporated in *Le Grand Meaulnes*, with a minimum of alterations, the most accomplished of the *Pays sans nom* extracts, an episode in which two young people discover a nest of dying chicks in a garden devastated by rain, and try to nurse them back to life in a desolate house through which the storm-winds moan.

Because he seems to have written few letters of consequence between August 1909 and the spring of 1910, we cannot date with accuracy his decision to abandon prose poetry and concentrate instead on a full-scale novel with characters, incidents, theme and plot. Between these dates, as is made clear in an undated, unpublished note, he set down his intention to write 'l'histoire d'un homme qui est en train d'écrire un roman. Les deux personnages sont: la femme qu'il aime et un homme qui lui ressemble mais il fait ce héros plus admirable qu'il ne l'est lui-même. Et cependant très vivant. Il l'imagine avec une précision extraordinaire'. In an extract from this early version, also undated and unpublished, the central character addresses himself to one of the several fictional representations of Yvonne de Quiévrecourt: 'Si vous étiez revenue quand vous deviez revenir, je n'aurais pas imaginé, écrit sur vous, Anne-Marie, ce roman'.

By 10 April 1910, his plans were sufficiently advanced for him to be able to announce to Rivière the names of his major characters, though he had still to decide on the hero: 'Je ne sais d'ailleurs pas encore si ce sera bien le grand Meaulnes le héros du livre — ou Seurel? ou Anne des Champs? ou moi, qui raconte' (7, p.338). The title of the novel was to have been *Le Jour des noces* and the main theme, the competing claims of human and divine love. Meaulnes, a moody and unpredictable young man, already in love with the elusive Anne-Marie des Champs, was to have been reunited with her in the course of a garden party beside the chapel of Sainte-Agathe, and to have married her soon after. A note in Alain-Fournier's skeletal synopsis specifies 'On les marie très jeunes'. Instead of exulting in his happiness, Meaulnes grows more and more morose, breaks down on his wedding-night and begs Anne-Marie to let him depart. He presumably renounces her for service to God because the next chapter is tentatively entitled 'Math. Meaulnes missionnaire'. Anne-Marie pines away and dies and the narrator, who remains distinct from all the other characters, is left at the end of the novel to meditate on events with Pierre Seurel, son of the widower schoolmaster of Epineuil. One or other of them would doubtless have pronounced the moral enunciated in the detailed summary Alain-Fournier sent to Rivière: 'Le jour où le bonheur indéniable, inéluctable, se dresse devant lui, et appuie contre le sien son visage humain, le grand Meaulnes s'enfuit non point par héroïsme mais par terreur, parce qu'il sait que la véritable joie n'est pas de ce monde' (ibid.).

This conclusion is highly symptomatic of Alain-Fournier's thinking throughout the summer of 1909 when he underwent an agonizing religious crisis from which he emerged disturbed but unconverted. His emotional responses and his literary plans were alike markedly influenced by several of the authors he particularly admired: Gide's *récit*, *La Porte étroite*, in which the heroine Alissa wastes away and dies rather than marry her beloved Jérôme, and Claudel's play *Partage de midi*, in which the hero Mesa can receive God's blessing only after being betrayed by the women he loves, both seemed to extol the virtues of ascetic renouncement. He was deeply affected by his reading of Dostoevsky's novel *The Idiot*, in which the epileptic hero's view of normal married pleasures is distinctly ambivalent. He

had also read *Moralités légendaires* by his youthful idol Jules
Laforgue, a set of stories in one of which Pierrot is too timid to
make love to his newly-won bride, Colombinette, and in another
of which, Lohengrin shrinks away from his wife on his wedding
night, embraces his pillow and implores it to bear him away.
Alain-Fournier's close familiarity with all these works may
explain how he came to conceive the dénouement he planned for
Le Jour des noces. It does not make that dénouement sound any
more credible in a setting he meant to make realistic ('C'est *le
pays sans nom* mais aussi le pays de tout le monde. Ce sera bien
plus humainement beau ainsi', ibid.). It might account, in part,
for the often criticized episode in *Le Grand Meaulnes* when the
hero deserts Yvonne de Galais the day after their wedding, but
the motives impelling that abrupt departure are of an entirely
different order. They were inspired by a painful and protracted
love-affair on which he embarked soon after the scenario for *Le
Jour des noces* was drawn up and before he seriously set to work
on it.

Not much is known about Jeanne Bruneau, other than that
she was a seamstress who lived with her sister in a small flat near
Notre Dame, and that she came from Bourges, in Alain-
Fournier's own native Cher *département* and where he once
briefly went to school. From the several letters he wrote to her
(*16*, pp.125-53), it is clear that theirs was a relationship founded
on intense physical attraction, characterized, at least intermittently, by periods of genuine tenderness; it is also clear that
on occasions he treated her with quite appalling harshness, his
principal cause of grievance being that she was not Yvonne de
Quiévrecourt. A regular cycle seems to have been established of
bitter recriminations, a melodramatic separation, a fond reconciliation, followed by recriminations, separation and reconciliation several times over. They seem to have found it as
painful to live apart as to live together until taking final leave of
each other in April 1912. The effect on Alain-Fournier's literary
plans was almost immediate: Jeanne and their affair were
promptly transposed into the still evolving novel. He wrote to
her in September 1910 after a weekend spent at the Normandy
farmhouse of the painter André Lhote: 'je travaille sans trêve,

plusieurs heures par jour à mon livre. Je pense terminer aujourd'hui le chapitre consacré à notre voyage d'Orgeville. Vous vous appellerez Annette'.

The chapter was duly written but subsequently quite drastically expurgated. In the earlier version, an extensive fragment of which was later published in *Miracles* (*4*, pp.211-17 and *1*, pp.192-95), all manner of explicit references make it quite clear that Annette is Meaulnes's mistress. In revising the material for final publication, Alain-Fournier proceeded methodically to establish that Meaulnes and Valentine were merely good friends. Most obviously, whereas, in the earlier version of the Orgeville episode, Meaulnes wakes up to find Annette sleeping in the same bed beside him, in the final version (p.161), she sleeps in a separate room. In that same early version, Meaulnes replies with a crisp 'Oui' to Annette's brutally direct: 'Qu'est-ce que vous voulez? Coucher avec moi?' In the final version, both question and answer are drastically attenuated:

> Est-ce que vous m'aimez, vous aussi? Vous aussi, vous allez me demander ma main?
> J'ai balbutié. Je ne sais pas ce que j'ai répondu. Peut-être ai-je dit: Oui. (p.160)

Also missing from the novel which was finally published in 1913 were any of the several attempts made in earlier versions to analyse Meaulnes's motives and his agonies of conscience, for example the narrator's wish to recapture 'l'amertume de sa voix et ce ton de regret qu'il prenait, l'angoisse de ce jeune homme tourmenté par deux désirs contraires — comme si vraiment on lui avait volé, et son effort pour conquérir ce paradis enfantin devait être à jamais vain'. One can only regret Alain-Fournier's decision not to follow up such promising leads. Whereas, in *Le Jour des noces*, Meaulnes was to have deserted his newly-married wife because of his preference — up until then, as far as one can judge, kept well hidden — for devotion to the Church, in *Le Grand Meaulnes*, his dilemma is, if not more agonizing, at any rate very much more credible. The 'jeune homme tourmenté

par deux désirs contraires' finds himself emotionally committed
to two women simultaneously: Yvonne de Galais, *la princesse
lointaine*, adored in his youth, who he thought was lost forever,
and Valentine Blondeau, responsive and accessible, with whom,
in spite of all their differences, he has fallen in love and for
whose well-being he has accepted full responsibility. In the final
novel, the narrator dismisses all this in two pithy sentences
(pp.167-68), and the reader is left to stage-manage in his own
mind what could and should have been a human drama of considerable intensity. Given the poignancy already in the situation,
it was arguably a gratuitous twist of the emotional screw for
Alain-Fournier to have made Valentine the former fiancée of
Yvonne's brother, Frantz.

Frantz de Galais was the last of the major characters to have
been invented and is a revealing example of Alain-Fournier's
creative technique. After being lured along so many false trails
at the instance of other writers, he decided that the surest way to
arrive at authenticity was to stay within the range of his own
experience. 'Je suis obligé de mettre exactement ce qui s'est
passé dans la réalité', he wrote in an unpublished letter of
August 1910, 'parce qu'alors je suis sûr que ce n'est pas du
fabriqué.' He reaffirmed this principle in a letter to Rivière in
September 1911: 'Je n'écris que sur la réalité. Tout ce que je
raconte se passe quelque part' (*7*, p.401). This definition of 'la
réalité' encompassed people, places and situations with which he
was personally familiar both in everyday life and in literature,
music and painting. Frantz is a case in point: in the few surviving
drafts in which he features he first appears as 'Willie, l'écolier
[or 'le bohémien'] anglais', a character whose acquaintance he
made in early boyhood at Epineuil, in the pages of a children's
magazine called *Le Petit Français illustré*, where he was
regularly represented as a stereotyped English public schoolboy,
with top hat and wing collar but, on one occasion, as the result
of some feat of derring-do, appeared hatless, with his head
heavily bandaged. He took his place in that gallery of equally
dauntless young heroes, such as Kipling's Kim and Stevenson's
Jim Hawkins, who were, for Alain-Fournier, such a distinctive
feature of the English adventure stories he never ceased to

admire. However, a more important model for Frantz de Galais was French, a former class-mate from Alain-Fournier's brief career at the naval *lycée* at Brest, who shot himself through the head in 1911 because of an unhappy love-affair, and is the central character in *Portrait*, the short story in Alain-Fournier's posthumously published *Miracles* (*4*, pp.199-210).

All the characters, places, events and situations in *Le Grand Meaulnes* were fashioned after the same formula, the different pieces sometimes deriving from notes on drafts of letters carefully hoarded over the years, sometimes being recalled directly through an effort of memory, and then being reassembled to form a new and autonomous entity (see *1*, pp.lxx-lxxxiv). However close the many parallels are between Alain-Fournier's life and *Le Grand Meaulnes*, it is nonetheless a fiction. There are significant divergences too. At the end of their first encounter, Yvonne de Galais promises Meaulnes that she will wait for him: Yvonne de Quiévrecourt promised Alain-Fournier no such thing. The fictitious Yvonne, in the final and early versions of the novel, dies wretchedly; the real-life Yvonne outlived him by half a century. By the time Alain-Fournier had reached the age of Seurel and Meaulnes, he had long since left Epineuil-le-Fleuriel and the tranquil centre of France. When they were half-heartedly ingesting their extravagantly elementary education, he was beginning enthusiastically to explore the French Symbolists and be captivated by Debussy. He may regularly have claimed to be *un paysan* but he was, in fact, a fashion-conscious and, culturally, most sophisticated Parisian. He became personally acquainted with most of the leading French writers of the day and, for some months in 1910, was private tutor to the young T.S. Eliot. From first to last he was a compulsive writer.

For all that, in the three main male characters of his one and only novel, he has bequeathed to us a spiritual self-portrait, true to the promise he made in a letter to Rivière in September 1910. Writing of his work in progress, he declared: 'là-dedans, il y aura tout moi; mes théories au passage et ce qui n'est pas mes théories; ce que j'aurais voulu faire et — tant pis! — ce que j'ai fait' (*7*, p.367). Meaulnes is Alain-Fournier as he would like to have been, charismatic, impulsive and, above all, irresistible to

Yvonne; Frantz de Galais is Alain-Fournier as he could be in both his best and worst moments, a dandy able to charm, indulged by all and sundry, querulous, petulant and more than a little spiteful when frustrated; Seurel is Alain-Fournier as circumstances obliged him to be, his fondest dreams forever frustrated, unable — and perhaps unwilling — to exorcize the ghosts from his past. Significantly, and altogether appropriately, it is to deprived and desolate Seurel that is entrusted the responsibility of telling the story and of answering, for both the titular hero and his creator, the question posed by Rimbaud on behalf of every nostalgic malcontent: 'N'eus-je pas une fois une jeunesse aimable, héroïque, fabuleuse, à écrire sur des feuilles d'or, trop de chance! Par quel crime, par quelle erreur ai-je mérité ma faiblesse actuelle?' ('Matin' in *Une Saison en enfer*).

2. The Narrator and his Narrative

Despite the title of the novel, it is not *primarily* a biography of Meaulnes. Too many basic questions about him remain unanswered. Only a few details are ever supplied of the life he led before he arrives in Sainte-Agathe on that cold Sunday afternoon in November and the motives for his coming there at all remain mysterious: his mother is said to be very wealthy (p.6), the Seurels' little school is in a remote village, fourteen kilometres distant from Meaulnes's home, and seems singularly ill-equipped to accommodate, let alone educate, a boarder in his late teens. We never learn about the life he leads after he deserts his newly-married wife or about how he reunited Frantz and Valentine. We are not given the slightest clue as to what has happened to him and his daughter in the years that have elapsed since he returned to Les Sablonnières to claim her, though the fact that Seurel now feels free to make public his private diary would suggest that both are dead. Even in the narrative that ostensibly concerns him, he is conspicuously absent for long stretches. The longer the narrative lasts, the less it seems to be about Meaulnes and the more it seems to be about the effect of Meaulnes and of Yvonne on Seurel, from whose consciousness we are seldom permitted to escape. In the following chapters, I shall analyse his distinctive fashion of reaction to and reporting on experience, and the ways in which he and the other characters interact. For the moment, my concern is how he orders the deceptively simple narrative.

Seurel's attitude towards that narrative is quite remarkably possessive. Other characters are occasionally allowed to relate stories — such knowledge as we have of Frantz's relationship with Valentine comes to us second or even third hand from other witnesses — but at the earliest possible opportunity, Seurel assumes authorial control. The account of Meaulnes's first discovery of *le domaine mystérieux* is provided not by the protagonist but by Seurel and, at the end of the novel, after presenting a few pages of Meaulnes's secret journal, Seurel insists on transcribing it. This explanation is both implausible and revealing: 'Il avait noté des souvenirs sur un séjour qu'ils avaient fait tous les deux à la campagne, je ne sais où. Mais, chose étrange, à partir de cet instant, peut-être par un sentiment de pudeur secrète, le journal était rédigé de façon si hâchée, si informe, griffonné si hâtivement aussi, que j'ai dû reprendre moi-même et reconstituer toute cette partie de son histoire' (pp.160-61). Seurel's characteristic vagueness about matters geographical — a point I shall return to later — is here matched by a cavalier disregard for editorial principles. A literary academic would have reproduced the original text, with all its imperfections, and supplied a commentary; so also would a mimetic novelist. Seurel is neither, and there are grounds for believing that he is motivated less by aesthetic than by moral principles. His presentation of the seventeen-year-old Jasmin Delouche is symptomatic. He recoils from him because 'il faisait l'homme; il répétait avec vanité ce qu'il entendait dire aux joueurs de billard, aux buveurs de vermouth' (p.22). Delouche's remarks are, one has to assume, about the subjects pub-drinkers were ever wont to talk about — politics, sport and sex; Seurel finds them so distasteful that he cannot record them. In reporting these — and, as we shall see, in speculating on more important subjects — he, like Meaulnes, is inhibited 'par un sentiment de pudeur secrète'. This prompts some crucial questions: how trustworthy is his memory? can we always trust his judgment? can we distinguish between fact and comment?

At least fifteen years have elapsed since the enactment of the drama that Seurel is recalling. At the very outset, he announces 'Nous avons quitté le pays depuis bientôt quinze ans' (p.3), and it is unlikely that the Seurels departed from Sainte-Agathe as soon as Meaulnes returned to Les Sablonnières. He has in his possession some letters and the journal written by Meaulnes, but gives no indication that he ever kept such a journal himself. He must, therefore, reconstruct past events partly from evidence provided by surviving witnesses but mainly through a sustained effort of recollection. He is quick to concede that his memory is fallible. After trying to recapture impressions of his very first sight of the Sainte-Agathe schoolhouse, ten years before Meaulnes arrives, he diffidently confesses:

> C'est ainsi, du moins, que j'imagine notre arrivée. Car aussitôt que je veux retrouver le lointain souvenir de cette première soirée d'attente dans notre cour de Sainte-Agathe, déjà ce sont d'autres attentes que je me rappelle; déjà, les deux mains appuyées aux barreaux du portail, je me vois épiant avec anxiété quelqu'un qui va descendre la grand-rue. Et si j'essaie d'imaginer la première nuit que je dus passer dans ma mansarde, au milieu des greniers du premier étage, déjà ce sont d'autres nuits que je me rappelle; je ne suis plus seul dans cette chambre; une grande ombre inquiète et amie passe le long des murs et se promène. Tout ce paysage paisible — l'école, le champ du père Martin, avec ses trois noyers, le jardin dès quatre heures envahi chaque jour par des femmes en visite — est à jamais, dans ma mémoire, agité, transformé par la présence de celui qui bouleversa toute notre adolescence et dont la fuite même ne nous a pas laissé de repos. (p.4)

Particularly noteworthy in this passage are the judicious selection of specific evocative details (to be compared with Alain-Fournier's letter to his parents about Epineuil quoted above, pp.11-12), the array of syntactical structures deployed to achieve maximum rhetorical effect (let there be rather less talk of Seurel's 'simple and straightforward' style!), his frank acknowledgement of an emotional fixation: Seurel is aware that there is another version of his past but, strive though he may, he is unable to recover it. Meaulnes, as we shall see, is more privileged. Like Proust's Marcel, he is granted more than one of those transcendental experiences when the senses are ravished, when Time's inexorable grip is relaxed and the far distant past restored unbidden.

There are other occasions when Seurel is well aware that his memory is defective. Although he can confidently reconstruct 'par le menu détail' the words he did *not* overhear exchanged between Meaulnes and Yvonne alone in their home immediately after the wedding (pp.136-39), he has a curiously patchy recollection of his first conversation with Yvonne after Meaulnes's dramatic departure: 'Elle parlait peu, mais elle disait chaque phrase avec une animation extraordinaire, comme si elle eût voulu se persuader à elle-même que le bonheur n'était pas évanoui encore... Je n'ai pas gardé le souvenir de ce que nous avons dit' (p.141). Of the countless conversations they have over the weeks and months that follow, when he seeks to console her for the absence of Meaulnes with the dubious strategy of never speaking about him, he retains only the most general of impressions: 'Je n'ai pas gardé d'autre souvenir que celui, à demi effacé déjà, d'un beau visage amaigri, de deux yeux dont les paupières s'abaissent lentement tandis qu'ils me regardent, comme pour déjà ne plus voir qu'un monde intérieur' (p.144).

On other occasions, however, when Seurel's memory clearly plays him false, he offers neither apology nor explanation. At the beginning of his narrative, he reveals that for much of his childhood, he was seriously disabled by coxalgia (p.8), an affliction of the hip (from the Greek *algos* 'pain' and the Latin *coxa* 'hip-bone'). All subsequent references to his disability speak of quite a different part of his anatomy: 'depuis long-temps, malgré mon mauvais genou' (p.111) and 'mon père m'emmenait dans l'Yonne, chez un spécialiste qui devait guérir mon genou' (p.113). After the commando-style raid on the snowbound school, when Meaulnes is ambushed and robbed of his map, Seurel professes to be baffled by the military efficiency of Frantz's troops: 'Où et comment les avait-il entraînés à la bataille? Voilà qui restait un mystère pour nous' (p.66). Yet, in terminology that consistently derives from the military register, he has already provided clear indications of the dramatic events in train: Seurel reports 'nous entendîmes des cris sur la route. C'était une bande de jeunes gens et de gamins, en colonne par quatre, au pas gymnastique, évoluant comme une compagnie parfaitement organisé, conduits par Delouche, Daniel, Giraudat, et un autre que nous ne connûmes point' (p.27); a few days later, 'nous entendions parfois des groupes de grands élèves qui s'arrêtaient un instant, comme par hasard, devant le grand

portail, le heurtaient en jouant à des jeux militaires
incompréhensibles et puis s'en allaient' (p.60).

While these particular lapses of memory may be of little consequence and may not place excessive strain on our credulity, the
same is not true of two other occasions when Seurel's temporary
amnesia crucially affects the whole course of the action. In the
account of his journey to *le domaine mystérieux*, Meaulnes
would seem to have made three separate references to the village
of Le Vieux-Nançay (p.32), and, while in the dining-hall at *la
fête étrange*, to have overheard a conversation between two
elderly ladies in which one is addressed as Moinelle (p.44). At
the time, mention of these names elicits no reaction whatsoever
from Seurel, even though Le Vieux-Nançay is the place he prizes
more than anywhere else on earth, and Moinel, an aunt of whom
he has always been fond, has a name so outlandish as to be
almost unique. There can be only two explanations for his
spectacular lack of reaction: either, because it is vital for the
unravelling of the plot for *le domaine* to remain *perdu*, Alain-
Fournier is relying on sleight of hand to deceive the reader, or,
because he has assumed control over Meaulnes's story years
after he heard it, Seurel is being wise after the event, and, as he
did with Meaulnes's allegedly illegible diary-entries, tidying up
the narrative, making clear what, at the time, either of the events
themselves or of their first re-telling, was imperfectly heard.
Since he evinces no interest in the mechanics or proprieties of
narratology, we have no way of telling.

If, over the data of his past, Seurel's memory cannot exercise
total recall, so, about characters and situations in his present, his
mind does not possess total knowledge. He is not the sort of
narrator who enjoys god-like omniscience; he is a dramatized
character, involved as much as any of the others in the action,
and, as we shall later see, capable of crucial misjudgments.
Occasionally he will frankly confess his ignorance. Imparting
the unlikely information that Delouche is still attending the
village school at the age of twenty, he comments: 'Il continuait,
je ne sais pourquoi, mais certainement sans aucun désir de
passer les examens, à suivre le cours supérieur' (p.100). Sometimes he will proffer what purports to be an explanation but

turns out to be no explanation at all. After Frantz and Ganache have fled from Sainte-Agathe in anticipation of the swoop by the local gendarmerie, Seurel wonders: 'comment Ganache avait-il pu à la fois dévaliser les basses-cours et guérir la bonne sœur pour la fièvre de son ami?' His answer to his own question is in no way enlightening: 'mais n'était-ce pas là toute l'histoire du pauvre diable? Voleur et chemineau d'un côté, bonne créature de l'autre' (p.85). In the course of the five months between Meaulnes's proposing to Yvonne de Galais and marrying her in the ruined chapel of Les Sablonnières, Seurel has become schoolmaster at the nearby hamlet of Saint-Benoist-des-Champs and Delouche a mason in his uncle's building business at Le Vieux-Nançay, the local village. Seurel comments: 'Ceci explique comment nous sommes là tous deux à rôder, vers quatre heures de l'après-midi, alors que les gens de la noce sont déjà tous repartis' (p.131). Seurel is well aware of the impropriety of their skulking outside the home into which the newly-married couple have retired — his choice of that pejorative verb *rôder* is revelatory (of what, we shall discuss later) — but he is at a loss to explain his behaviour. The *comment* information which is provided is less interesting than the *pourquoi* information which is concealed.

No less tantalizing are a number of details which the narrator never explains. When, at *la fête étrange*, Yvonne de Galais reveals her name to Meaulnes, he says, after they have been briefly separated:

Le nom que je vous donnais était plus beau.
—Comment? Quel était ce nom? fit-elle, toujours avec la même gravité. Mais il eut peur d'avoir dit une sottise et ne répondit rien. (p.51)

That name is never divulged: whatever it is, it cannot be the 'Mélisande' Alain-Fournier thought of bestowing on Yvonne de Quiévrecourt because Debussy's opera was not performed until 1903, some years after the events in Seurel's narrative which, in the very opening line, he pointedly places in the 1890s.

The consistently undervalued — and, as I shall later argue,

regularly misrepresented — figure of Jasmin Delouche provides snippets of information, which turn out to be of crucial importance but which are never adequately explained. When Meaulnes leaves Sainte-Agathe for Paris to pursue his hopeless quest of the lost domain, the grieving Seurel seeks consolation and companionship by describing *la fête étrange* to some of the other schoolboys:

> Est-ce que je raconte mal cette histoire? Elle ne produit pas l'effet que j'attendais.
> Mes compagnons, en bons villageois qui rien n'étonne, ne sont pas surpris pour si peu.
> C'était une noce, quoi! dit Boujardon.
> Delouche en a vu une, à Préveranges, qui était plus curieuse encore. (pp.94-95)

So closely have we been obliged to identify with the narrator's point of view that we are inclined, as like as not, to dismiss the village-boys' comments as obtuse or inconsequential. Seurel certainly does so and, borne along on the flow of his narrative, we have, for the moment, no option but to follow. Later reflection suggests that he and we could be wrong. The instinctive reaction of 'le gros Boujardon' to the details of *la fête étrange* is not so very different from that of 'le grand Meaulnes' when he first sees the guests arriving: 'Il s'agit d'une noce, sans doute, se dit Augustin' (p.36). For his part, Delouche may conceivably be exaggerating but, as subsequent events establish, he is not in the habit of lying. There are a number of references to Préveranges which establish it as a place of some importance: there is a château there, with its pack of hunting hounds (p.121), it provides the mid-wife to deliver Yvonne's baby daughter (p.149) and the priest to administer the last rites (p.151). Evidently, it must be relatively close to Les Sablonnières — the road between the two runs past Frantz's little house (p.142) — but how close it is, and in what direction, we are never told. This is wholly characteristic of the geography of the narrative which remains conspicuously imprecise throughout (see *19*). The few statistics that are provided are quite unhelpful. Meaulnes, we are

told, departs from *le domaine mystérieux* in a *berline* coach at
midnight and arrives, six kilometres west of Sainte-Agathe at
four o'clock that morning (p.86). Unfortunately, since he sleeps
for the duration of the journey, and none of us knows how
often, or for how long, the coach stopped along the way, we are
even less equipped than he is to draw a map of the region. Even
when the domain has been located and most of the mysteries
resolved, we still lack the information we would require to locate
the villages in space. If he sets out from his Uncle Florentin's
shop at Le Vieux-Nançay at 4 a.m., Seurel assures us that he can
cycle on to Sainte-Agathe in time for lunch and then ride a
further fourteen kilometres to reach La Ferté-d'Angillon, the
village of both Meaulnes and Aunt Moinel, before night falls in
late August (p.110). The only other statistics he provides are that
Vierzon, the nearest railway station to Sainte-Agathe, is three
kilometres away, and that it takes him three quarters of an hour
to walk across the fields from his school at Saint-Benoist to Les
Sablonnières. As an array of 'facts', it is unlikely to impress the
professional geographer or any pupil from the school of
Gradgrind, but the very imprecision performs two important
functions in the narrative: it helps to characterize *l'univers
imaginaire* of the untravelled and romantically-minded narrator,
to whom any village beyond the immediate horizon seems to be
at the far ends of the earth, and it underlines the irony of the
plot which requires that everyone should all along know where
to find *le domaine perdu* except Meaulnes and Seurel.

Delouche has a major role to play in this ironic strategy, and
another area left tantalizingly vague in the narrative, is his
relationship with the gamekeeper Baladier. Immediately after
Frantz flees from the gendarmes, on a glorious spring morning
which seems to promise that all their dreams might still come
true, Meaulnes and Seurel set out separately to find the lost
domain. Seurel's hopes are high as he marches through *le bois
des Communaux* but are promptly dashed when he reaches the
far perimeter and finds himself in front of Baladier's lodge. He
turns back, deflated, assuming the quest has once again come to
a dead-end (pp.88-89). His judgment is once again at fault. That
same game-keeper turns out to have connections both with

Seurel's uncle Florentin and with Delouche, and to have been instrumental in securing Delouche's invitation to the garden-party at Les Aubiers farm where Meaulnes is reunited with Yvonne (p.121). There are grounds for supposing that he is the very game-keeper who once took Delouche on a conducted tour round the Galais estate (p.103), but on this point Seurel stays silent. One cannot be sure whether Alain-Fournier is here being careless or whether his narrator is being obtuse. If it is the latter, it would not be for the first time. The closer one studies his narrative, the warier one is bound to become.

There are moments when, purportedly transcribing the evidence of stress, Seurel, more or less overtly, smuggles in a comment of his own. When he is describing the exchanges between Meaulnes and Yvonne, alone at last after their wedding, just before Frantz's fateful owl-call signal: 'il s'approcha d'Yvonne et, très légèrement, il mit sa main sur son épaule. Elle sentit doucement peser auprès de son cou cette caresse à laquelle il aurait fallu savoir répondre' (p.137). Various questions arise: what would an appropriate response have been? in which consciousness is the awareness of deprivation: that of Meaulnes? or of Seurel? If, as seems most likely, it is the latter, how has he come by the data? Given the marked dearth of opportunities to discuss the subject to which, soon after, he pointedly draws our attention, it can hardly have been Yvonne. And, since Meaulnes runs away next morning, it can scarcely be him either. Is Seurel, therefore, recording fact or indulging, surreptitiously, in speculation?

In one area in particular, the obtrusion of Seurel's idio-syncratic views is very much more overt: this is the contentious matter of Meaulnes's attitude to happiness. In the shadows, close by the house of the newly-married couple, Seurel lurks listening. On the mist-laden wind come the notes of a piano. He translates what he takes to be its message: 'C'est d'abord comme une voix tremblante qui, de très loin, ose à peine chanter sa joie... C'est comme le rire d'une petite fille qui dans sa chambre, a été chercher tous ses jouets et les répand devant son ami... Je pense aussi à la joie craintive encore d'une femme qui a été mettre une belle robe et qui vient la montrer et ne sait pas si elle plaira... Cet air que je ne connais pas, c'est aussi une prière, une supplication au bonheur de ne pas être trop cruel, un salut et comme un agenouillement devant le bonheur...' (p.132). Whether the piano music triggers such a plethora of associations in Meaulnes's imagination we never know because, from first to last, we are enclosed within the consciousness of Seurel: the laughter of the little girl, the uncertainty of the woman, the concept of a happiness too fearful to contemplate are in his mind and nowhere else at this moment. These are not the only signals of his heightened emotions on the day of the wedding. His brief account of the events leading up to the wedding is prefaced by the following eloquent utterance:

> Pour celui qui ne veut pas être heureux, il n'a qu'à monter dans son grenier et il entendra, jusqu'au soir, siffler et gémir les naufrages; il n'a qu'à s'en aller dehors, sur la route, et le vent lui rabattra son foulard sur la bouche comme un chaud baiser soudain qui le fera pleurer. Mais pour celui qui aime le bonheur, il y a au bord d'un chemin boueux, la maison des Sablonnières, où mon ami Meaulnes est rentré avec Yvonne de Galais, qui est sa femme depuis midi. (p.130)

As a sample of epithalamium, or marriage-hymn, this is somewhat less than orthodox. Distress is much more prominent than delight: the intensity of the writing has been channelled into the first sentence; the second is markedly more perfunctory, and the euphoria it purports to express is subversively undercut by what seems the gratuitous reference to mud (reminiscent of that sinister last line in Rimbaud's poem 'Mémoire' which finally destroys the vision of evanescent childhood happiness which preceded it). Seurel does not speak in his own person and does not overtly identify with the imaginary bystander exulting in the happiness of the bridal pair. The very least that can be inferred is that he feels strongly for and with the hypothetical twin, so emotionally disorientated that he hears the sound of shipwrecks in the land-locked centre of France and feels a burning kiss on his lips in frozen February. It is surely not without significance that the closer Meaulnes and Yvonne approach to their wedding-bed, the more disturbed Seurel becomes, and the more he insists on attributing to Meaulnes the holy dread he evidently feels at the physical realities of marriage he cannot bring himself to contemplate. Is it because he prefers to believe that they have somehow remained young and virginal that he persists in calling Meaulnes's wife 'Mlle de Galais' (p.136), and in thinking of his own mother, to whom he otherwise displays the meekest possible respect, as 'Millie'? (p.3).

Be that as it may, Seurel persists in suggesting that Meaulnes must have run away from his newly-wed wife because of fear. He speculates on his possible reactions to the repeated owl-call signals of the insistent Frantz: 'Que se passa-t-il alors dans ce cœur obscur et sauvage? Je me le suis souvent demandé et je ne l'ai su que lorsqu'il fut trop tard. Remords ignorés? Regrets inexplicables? Peur de voir s'évanouir bientôt entre ses mains ce bonheur inouï qu'il tenait si serré? Et alors tentation terrible de jeter irrémédiablement à terre, tout de suite, cette merveille qu'il avait conquise?' (p.137). Having mooted the possibility that Meaulnes might well have run away because he fears disillusion-ment — the only explanation which, we later learn, makes sense to Yvonne — he returns to the charge that he fears happiness itself. The concept is expressed not in a litany of sentimental conceits, but in a single powerful, if obscure, image in which happiness is represented as an unrelenting gaoler or some pur-suing animal (like Francis Thompson's 'Hound of Heaven'): 'Il avait fallu que mon grand compagnon échappât à la fin à son bonheur tenace...' (p.140). All of this, however, is essentially neither here nor there. The point that needs to be made about Seurel's speculations on Meaulnes's reason for running away is that they are nonsense: Meaulnes is driven to desert Yvonne after the wedding, not by fear of happiness, or the prospect of disenchantment, but by corrosive guilt and his outraged sense of honour. An even more important point that needs to be made is that Seurel knows full well that his speculations are nonsensical even as he goes through the motions of speculating. Why he elects to behave in this fashion is the very essence of his narrative technique.

When he begins to narrate the events, so long after they have happened, Seurel already knows their outcome: he knows where Meaulnes went when he disappeared so dramatically from school, he knows the true identity of the young stranger with the bandaged head, the lost domain has been found and supplied with its missing name, Meaulnes has become engaged to Valentine and Yvonne in rapid succession, Yvonne has died, he himself has carried her corpse out to the hearse, he has lived for a year in what survived of the château which was once so remote, the secrets of Meaulnes's diary have been discovered and digested, Valentine and Frantz have been reunited, Meaulnes has returned to claim his daughter — all this knowledge is in the narrator's gift when he bids to button-hole his reader with that unemphatic opening sentence 'Il arriva chez nous un dimanche de novembre 189..' (p.3). To keep that reader in thrall, Seurel consistently conceals all that he knows, and he pretends to share the reader's ignorance. Rare indeed are the instances when he breaks his self-imposed code of make-believe, and grudgingly concedes that he has access to privileged information: characteristically, having revealed that he subsequently discovered why Meaulnes deserted Yvonne — 'Je me le suis souvent demandé et je ne l'ai su que lorsqu'il fut trop tard' (p.137) — he promptly proceeds to list the alternative explanations which occurred to him at the time of Meaulnes's flight, all of which turn out to be false. His narrative formula throughout is to reproduce in all their immediacy his reactions to characters, events and situations. It is a technique admirably suited for conveying suspense, surprise, bafflement, wonder and shock, and it is in these areas, rather than those of analysis and explanation, that Seurel is positively masterful. In Part I especially his narrative performance is that of a virtuoso.

His sense of timing is exquisite: he exploits to the full the always rich potential of delaying the solution to the riddles he himself has posed. The opening word of the narrative is the pronoun 'Il', and the momentous impact of that 'il' on everyone around him is very soon made manifest: try though he might to escape back into a more distant past, the narrator is held prisoner. The 'il' assumes a shape, 'une grande ombre inquiète et amie' (p.4), the epithets selected to characterize its qualities being as suggestive as the noun that designates its form. Eloquent signals of cataclysm are next conveyed by verbs: 'Tout ce paysage paisible... est à jamais, dans ma mémoire, agité, transformé par la présence de celui qui bouleversa notre adolescence et dont la fuite même ne nous a pas laissé de repos' (p.4). Although this disruptive figure is now promptly named as 'Meaulnes', his arrival on the scene is further delayed. His mother appears, providing further evidence of her son's disruptive influence with her 'visage maigre et fin, mais ravagé par l'inquiétude' (p.5), and a foretaste of his wilfulness with the first of the few words we ever hear her utter: 'Où est-il passé? mon Dieu!... Il était avec moi tout à l'heure. Il a déjà fait le tour de la maison. Il s'est peut-être sauvé...' (p.5). Meaulnes's emergence is further delayed, until after his mother has related some of his escapades with 'un air supérieur et mystérieux qui nous intrigua' (p.6), and until after his footsteps have been heard from the room above which are evoked with adjectives we will come to recognize as Seurel's stock in trade: 'Au-dessus de nous... un pas inconnu, assuré, allait et venait, ébranlant le plafond, traversait les immenses greniers ténébreux du premier étage et se perdait enfin vers les chambres d'adjoints abandonnés...' (p.7). When, after this atmospheric build-up, Meaulnes finally appears 'dans l'entrée obscure de la salle à manger' (p.7), he does not disappoint the narrator's expectations: he pointedly ignores the adults, unhesitatingly addresses Seurel in the familiar form of the second person, produces an unexploded firework nobody else has previously noticed in the upstairs attics, and expertly lights it with one of his own matches. The emphasis on loneliness and gloom which has been accumulating throughout the opening chapter is dispelled as Meaulnes and Seurel stand hand in hand, unflinching, in a coruscation of red and white stars.

The narrator stage-manages the rest of the events in Part I with the same sure touch so evident in his initial presentation of Meaulnes, providing just enough to arouse the reader's curiosity but taking his time to satisfy it. There is the seemingly incon-sequential scene in the Desnoues' forge, where each icy winter's evening, the blacksmith puts on his own firework display of incandescent sparks, and unwittingly shows Meaulnes the road to adventure and the means of travelling it. Through Seurel's eyes, we see Meaulnes departing with the borrowed horse and cart, the return of the empty cart hours later 'telle une épave qu'eût ramenée la haute mer' (p.18), and the reappearance of Meaulnes after three days' absence, with wisps of straw about his person 'et surtout son air de voyageur fatigué, affamé, mais émerveillé' (p.20). Where he has been and what he has done are questions not immediately answered. We have to be further teased by a glimpse of the old-fashioned silk waistcoat with mother-of-pearl buttons, by the regularly repeated drama of Meaulnes tormentedly pacing back and forth through the gloomy attics, or preparing to set out, fully dressed in the middle of the night, for 'ce pays mystérieux où une fois déjà il s'était évadé' (pp.25-26). Only after our expectations have been thoroughly aroused does Seurel finally condescend to recount Meaulnes's story.

The narrative now becomes third-person but the technique remains the same: perceptions are registered with the maximum of precision and the minimum of explanation: cumulatively they generate an irresistible effect of mystery and magic. The stages by which Meaulnes loses contact with the familiar world of Sainte-Agathe are charted just as tellingly as the preparations for his first appearance. As Claude Vincenot indicates in his perceptive analysis of this section of the novel (*39*, p.270), in a clear December landscape glittering with hoar-frost, the roads grow progressively narrower and rougher: 'la route de Vierzon' becomes 'plus étroite et mal empierrée' then 'un étroit chemin défoncé' next a 'sentier raviné', in which 'il y avait... tout juste passage pour la voiture', then 'un chemin' blocked by a stream in spate, followed by a 'sentier', a 'sente' and a mere 'passage' until total darkness descends and Meaulnes is lost in the midst of trackless fields. Any emphatic reader must so keenly share his sense of disorientation at this point that it is almost superfluous for Seurel to comment: 'Ainsi peu à peu s'embrouillait la piste du grand Meaulnes et se brisait le lien qui l'attachait à ceux qu'il avait quittés' (pp.28-34).

When, with his knee damaged by a blow from a wheel of his now vanished cart, he limps throughout the next day across the desolate Sologne heathland and literally stumbles into *le domaine mystérieux*, his perceptions are noted with both precision and concision. Uncertain what the grey spire signifies, rising from a wood of fir-trees, he takes it to be either 'quelque vieux manoir abandonné' or 'quelque pigeonnier désert' (p.35); in the darkness he conceives three rather different identities for the main building 'ferme, château ou abbaye' (p.41), but does not single out any one of them; the closest approximation he can make of the grounds surrounding the building is 'une sorte de grande cour-jardin' (p.42). Events, scenes and characters follow one another with vertiginous rapidity and in meaningless sequence: as he takes cover in the bushes, children's voices are heard in disembodied chorus, one of which speaks of a yellow pony, another of a boat-trip, while three separate voices in rapid succession trill variations on the theme that this is a kingdom where children rule; a courtyard is jammed full with coaches of every type and vintage; what he anticipates will be a hay-loft proves to be a vast bedroom, its mantelpiece and armchairs covered with vases, costly antiques and ancient weapons; a large bed, behind a curtain in the alcove, is strewn with gilt-bound books, lutes with broken strings and candelabra; wistful piano music is heard in the distance interspersed with the whining of the wind; a fat man, clad in a vast overcoat and bearing a pole hung with multicoloured lanterns, insists that Wellington was an American; the bedroom floor is dotted with grit that crunches underfoot, the drive leading to the main building is swept as clean as a well-kept carpet; a fifteen year old, dressed like an English public schoolboy, struts past on the very tips of his toes; tiny boys and girls play in one room, elderly men and women dine in another; one old woman calmly accuses her companion of being as mad as ever and is told, just as placidly, that she is incurably pig-headed; hordes of squeaking children are pursued along seemingly endless corridors by a loping Pierrot trailing long white sleeves, other children dance stately measures, still others watch a magic lantern show, yet others sit silently, turning the pages of huge picture-books, while Meaulnes sits listening to a young woman playing a piano, imagining she is his wife; next day, on a day stolen from spring, this same girl tells Meaulnes her name and promises that she will wait for him to return.

I shall return to *la fête étrange* in chapter 5, to examine its significance and the role it plays in the totality of the novel. Here, my concern is the way the narrator weaves the spell which normally charms even those readers who remain resistant to the rest of his blandishments. It is due, in part, to the judicious placing of his relatively small stock of images and to the suavity and subtle rhythms of his prose (stirring the emotions in a way that my bald summary assuredly does not) but, it is due, most of all, to the juxtaposition of disparate details, presented with the minimum of speculation or explanation. By this, pre-eminently, without recourse to magic potions or fabulist's sleight of hand, we are transported into a world compounded of 'real life' elements but no less enchanted than the 'faery lands forlorn' of Thomas the Rhymer or La Belle Dame sans merci.

Some of the other techniques which the narrator exploits with comparable success have already received their fair measure of critical attention. They include his switching from the past tense into the historic present for periods of particularly heightened emotion (the chapters 'L'Evasion', 'Le Jour des noces' and Seurel's contemplating the dead Yvonne), the consistent use of *points de suspension* and a whole array of chapter-endings which make their particular point, be it suspense or pathos, as effectively as the last line of a successful sonnet. One other feature, however, has been largely overlooked, and this is the narrator's idiosyncratic ordering of the chronology of events. In keeping with his policy of trying to communicate how these were registered in his consciousness at the moment of perception, he arranges them not in the sequence in which they actually occurred but in the order in which they really affect him. The consequences can turn out to be surprising to the reader and conceivably were unforeseen by the narrator: Meaulnes's experiences on the way to and at *la fête étrange* took place in December but are not related until the following February: the still-to-be-identified Frantz de Galais accordingly makes a discreet first appearance in Sainte-Agathe (p.27), in advance of his attempted suicide (p.58). Meaulnes has already fallen in love with Valentine, become engaged to her and then deserted her well before Delouche points Seurel in the direction of *le domaine mystérieux*; the story of his spiritual decline and fall is not related until after his marriage, his dramatic departure and Yvonne's agonizing death. The narrative effectiveness of this particular dislocation of the time-sequence is, at the very least, debatable.

Two time-scales operate throughout the novel, one measured by the clock and the calendar, the other registered by and through the consciousness of Seurel: it will prove instructive to consider both. Because he makes a regular point of noting the season, if not the precise day of the month, we can date the events with reasonable confidence. Almost four years elapse between Meaulnes's first arrival in Sainte-Agathe one Sunday afternoon in November 189-, and his return to Les Sablonnières and his one-year-old baby daughter on a Sunday morning in late September. For Meaulnes, those four years have been packed with action: less than a month after his first arrival at Sainte-Agathe, Meaulnes participates in *la fête étrange*; six months later, after he has moved on to Paris, he is told that Yvonne is married; within a year of hearing that news on 14 June, he becomes engaged to Valentine; on 17 June, he discovers she is the ex-fiancée of Frantz de Galais, and they separate; on 25 August, ne visits Bourges hoping for a reunion; before the end of that same month, he proposes to Yvonne and is accepted; the wedding takes place the following February; the day after the wedding, he runs away; Yvonne gives birth to her baby daughter that September and dies; he returns the following September with Valentine and Frantz, who has failed to keep the tryst made with Seurel for the February of that year. Many readers will, I suspect, have felt that these events are spread out over a much greater span of time. This is likely to be even truer of the impression we probably form of Frantz de Galais's stay in Sainte-Agathe.

Frantz has arrived in the locality and is already drilling his schoolboy troops by 15 February (pp.26-27). The raid on the schoolhouse is carried out on 'un jeudi soir, vers la fin du mois' (p.60). The following morning, to Seurel's astonishment, the young leader with heavily bandaged head takes his place in M. Seurel's classroom; apparently he is not called upon to divulge his name or even to invent an alias. In the course of the same day, he takes part in the joust in the school playground, is later assaulted by some of his own troops and is warned that he must stay behind when lessons have ended to help sweep out the class-room because 'les nouveaux étaient toujours désignés d'office pour faire le second balayeur, le jour de leur arrivée' (p.72). In the course of the sweeping operation, he makes the pact with Meaulnes and Seurel, and they swear the solemn oath to come to his aid whenever he summons them; the pact seems to be uni-lateral, there is no reciprocal pledge made by him (p.75). He then departs, is taken ill, remains incommunicado for three days, recovers sufficiently to perform before the villagers when he removes his bandage and allows Meaulnes to see his true identity. He is secure within his caravan before Meaulnes can push through the crowd to speak to him there and then, and steals away that night before Meaulnes has the chance of questioning him further. He has attended the school for just one day, and been on friendly, conversational terms with Meaulnes and Seurel for little more than an hour in all!

If the reader assumes otherwise (and I have been misled on this matter for longer than I dare admit!) it must be, in large measure, because the amount of space devoted to events in the narrative is determined more by the dramatic or the emotional charge they are felt to hold by Seurel than by the time needed to enact them as measured by calendar or clock. To the four days occupied by Meaulnes's journey to and experiences at the lost domain, Seurel devotes some thirty-one pages (pp.28-59); on the five days between Frantz's theft of Meaulnes's map and his escape from the gendarmes, he provides twenty-three pages (pp.60-83). On the other hand, the five months which elapse between Meaulnes's proposal to Yvonne and their wedding are despatched in a paragraph so cursory that we know nothing of where he lives, how he spends his days nor the agonies of guilt he is presumably suffering over Valentine. Yvonne, we must presume, goes to her grave knowing nothing of her husband's secret, so he may not entirely have placated the conscience which is, in part, assuaged by his reuniting Valentine with Frantz: the nineteen months of activity which have brought this about, Seurel dismisses in just seven words.

Seurel's subjective experience of Time is expressed not only through the uneven distribution of his narrative energy but by categoric utterances which are positively misleading. Having retold Meaulnes's story of *la fête étrange* in his own words, he continues: 'Le grand vent et le froid, la pluie ou la neige, l'impossibilité où nous étions de mener à bien de longues recherches nous empêchèrent, Meaulnes et moi, de reparler du Pays perdu avant la fin de l'hiver. Nous ne pouvions rien commencer de sérieux, durant ces brèves journées de février, ces jeudis sillonnés de bourrasques, qui finissaient régulièrement vers cinq heures par une morne pluie glacée' (p.60). This powerfully conveys a sense of chronic frustration spread over a considerable period. At the same time, it does not square with facts he goes out of his way to highlight: he specifies that Meaulnes began to tell his story 'une nuit, vers le 15 février' (p.26) and adds shortly after, 'mon compagnon ne me conta pas cette nuit-là tout ce qui lui était arrivé sur la route' (p.28); Frantz sets his ambush and steals the map 'un jeudi soir, vers la fin du mois' (p.60) and reveals his identity at the circus performance four days later at the beginning of March (p.78); the very next day, after Frantz's abrupt departure, Meaulnes and Seurel set out on foot to look for the lost domain, fail to find it and that same evening, Meaulnes, equally abruptly, decides to depart: 'Apprends-le, Seurel: j'ai écrit à ma mère jeudi dernier, pour lui demander de finir mes études à Paris. C'est aujourd'hui que je pars' (p.92). He is as good as his word. Seurel's word is another matter. Of Meaulnes's romantic adventure, the narration of which was begun but not completed on 15 February, Seurel declares: 'ce resta longtemps le grand secret de nos adolescences' (*sic*, p.28). Within a month, Meaulnes sets out for Paris early in the afternoon; before night has fallen, Seurel reveals that great secret of his adolescence to the unimpressed village boys.

Together with the misjudgments of Meaulnes's motives, these

inaccurate pronouncements about the passage of time are merely
the more obvious instances of the narrator's being contradicted
by his own narrative. This purports to be the chronicle of some-
one else's adventures but it turns out to be an exercise in self-
portraiture. Even the choice of title is both misleading and
symptomatic, expressing the narrator's adulation of the figure
he has cast as his hero and his own exaggerated modesty. In fact,
so indelible on the narrative is the imprint of the narrator's
personality that it could, perfectly appropriately, have borne the
title *Le Petit Seurel*.

3. Vision and Voice

Just as Seurel is not always trustworthy as a narrator so, as observer and reporter, he is seldom neutral. His very particular vision of the world and of experience, his hopes, fears, predilections and prejudices are regularly revealed not only through his choice of words and images but also through his syntax and sentence-structure. For example, in what is still the outstanding study of the stylistic features of *Le Grand Meaulnes*, G. Timmermans draws attention to the increase achieved in emotional intensity by beginning a sentence with the simple conjunction 'Et'. The narrator is inordinately fond of using this device at the end of a chapter or dramatic episode; it suggests a brief, dramatic pause in the flow of the narrative, as though the narrator were selecting his words with extra special care, and the effect is, almost invariably, to highlight or put the final gloss on what has gone before: 'Et le soir, au dîner, il y eut, à la table de famille, un compagnon silencieux...' (p.8); 'Et c'est là que tout commença, environ huit jours avant Noël' (p.10); 'Et j'y ai souvent repensé depuis' (p.13); 'Et c'est ainsi qu'il quitta, refermant soigneusement la porte, ce mystérieux endroit...' (p.56); 'Et c'est tout ce que je me rappelle de cette morne fin d'un grand jour de défaite' (p.90. See *36*, pp.73-74 and 86-87).

Another favourite device is delaying the introduction of the subject of the sentence either by placing it after its verb or by beginning the sentence with adverbial clauses of space or time. The effect, this time, is a heightening of curiosity or suspense: 'Enfin glissa lentement, entre les rideaux, la face — sillonnée de rides, tout écarquillée tantôt par la gaieté tantôt par la détresse, et semée de pains à cacheter! — d'un long pierrot...' (p.81); 'En effet, assis sur une pile du pont des Glacis, nous attendait le grand Meaulnes' (p.90); 'A la porte vitrée s'arrêtaient et s'égouttaient, dans le brouillard de septembre, des charrettes, venues du fond de la campagne' (p.105).

Timmermans' essay contains the most searching study so far attempted of the musical qualities of the prose of *Le Grand Meaulnes*. He singles out for particular praise the discreet use of alliteration: 'tout ce paysage paisible' (p.4); 'il montrait dans ses paroles et ses gestes le mépris le plus parfait pour sa propre personne' (p.39); 'après cette fête où tout était charmant, mais fiévreux ou fou' (p.46); 'la branlante barrière de bois qui entourait le vivier' (p.46); 'C'était le commencement du désarroi et de la dévastation' (p.55); 'il passa près du vivier où le matin même il s'était miré...' (p.55). He provides, with a wealth of examples too detailed even to summarize here, a most sensitive analysis of the rhythms and harmonies of units as short as the phrase and as long as the sentence (*36*, pp.66-69 and 76-87). It is impossible to study his examples and remain unpersuaded by his final conclusion that 'la prose vraiment poétique est une affaire d'oreille autant que de cœur et surtout une affaire d'oreille avant une affaire de cœur' (*36*, p.89). But the auditory sense is by no means the only one to which the narrative appeals.

Seurel registers his perceptions of his quiet country environment with marvellous sharpness and concision: 'sur la route blanchie de givre, les petits oiseaux tourbillonnaient autour des pieds de l'âne trottinant' (p.17); 'Parfois une branche morte de la haie se prenait dans la roue et se cassait avec un bruit sec...' (p.30); 'Il y a tout juste une branche de rosier sans feuilles qui cogne la vitre, du côté de la lande' (p.136). He responds as readily to the smell of 'les harengs grillés sur le poêle et la laine roussie de ceux qui, en entrant, se sont chauffés de trop près' (p.13) as he does to the sight of 'les bauges des lièvres et les petits sillons de sable où les lapins ont gratté fraîchement... un collet tendu... la trace d'un braconnier...' (p.131). He notes the distinctive indications of the passage of the seasons. Pupils arrive in their classroom from the countryside in winter: 'Ils arrivaient tout éblouis encore d'avoir traversé des paysages de givre, d'avoir vu les étangs glacés, les taillis où les lièvres détalent... Il y avait dans leurs blouses un goût de foin et d'écurie qui alourdissait l'air de la classe, quand ils se pressaient autour du poêle rouge. Et ce matin-là, l'un d'eux avait apporté dans un panier un écureuil gelé qu'il avait découvert en route. Il essayait, je me souviens, d'accrocher par ses griffes, au poteau du préau, la longue bête raidie...' (pp.19-20). He welcomes the arrival of the spring: 'Une brise délicieuse comme une eau tiédie coulait par-dessus le mur; une pluie silencieuse avait mouillé la nuit les feuilles des pivoines; la terre remuée du jardin avait un goût puissant, et j'entendais, dans l'arbre voisin de la fenêtre, un oiseau qui essayait d'apprendre la musique...' (p.78). With the same judicious choice of specific detail, he evokes the manifold activities of a boyhood spent in a remote village in the very centre of France before the arrival of the motor car, the telephone, the radio or television. While he pays scant attention to the mechanics of teaching and learning, his senses nonetheless register the sights, sounds and smells of the schoolroom, and there is no shortage of detail about the village-boys' leisure activities: they visit farm-buildings, see cows being milked, watch the blacksmith at work in his forge, go bird-nesting in spring and for riverside picnics in summer, they scuffle and joust in the school playground, they consume sweets and lemonade illicitly in the back room of the village shop.

Every so often, there is a brief but sharp-edged glimpse of the grown-up country folk at work or play: 'De temps à autre, dans la rue, passait une dame du village, la tête baissée à cause du vent' (p.12); 'Le maréchal laissait à petits coups pesants et clairs retomber son marteau sur l'enclume' (p.12). So deceptively simple and artless do these notations seem that we might just be tempted to accept Seurel's view of himself as 'un gamin du bourg pareil aux autres' (p.93). Not for the first time, however, his judgment is in error. Very few 'gamins du bourg' can have his artistic eye for graphic detail or his poetic gift for placing 'the *best* words in the best order': consider the lovely line, deservedly singled out for praise by Henri Gillet (*12*, p.312), 'Et sur cette solitude parfaite brillait un soleil de décembre clair et glacial' (p.35). And fewer still, one suspects, share his sense that this quiet and secluded countryside is charged with mystery and menace.

To communicate this, he employs a number of techniques. As Stephen Ullman demonstrates in a perceptive study (*38*, pp.99-123), the use of imagery in the novel is 'discreet and unobtrusive'. The narrator prefers explicit simile to implicit metaphor and, remaining consistent with the narrator's country upbringing, analogies are drawn most commonly from rural life: 'elle enleva sa coiffure, et, durant toute la scène qui suivit, elle la tint contre sa poitrine, renversée comme un nid dans son bras droit replié' (p.6); 'je ne reconnaissais plus la femme aux cheveux gris, que j'avais vue courbée devant la porte, une minute auparavant, avec cet air suppliant et hagard de poule qui aurait perdu l'oiseau sauvage de sa couvée' (p.6); 'quelques vieilles paysannes avec de rondes figures ridées comme des pommes' (p.43). The largest number of the analogies in the narrative are of this category — comparisons with birds, running water or country customs — but there is an array of others, rather fewer in number, but more exotic in their range of reference and more dramatic in their effect: these all evoke the sea.

There are three motifs. The theme of adventure is likened to the breaking of waves: the very first image in the novel is of the Sainte-Agathe schoolhouse, remembered as the 'demeure d'où partirent et où revinrent se briser, comme des vagues sur un rocher désert, nos aventures' (p.3). The second motif is of shipwreck and drowning: the farmer's horse and cart, brought back without Meaulnes, are likened to 'une épave qu'eût ramenée la haute mer' (p.47), while for Seurel, locked outside the home of his newly-married friends, the moaning of the wind evokes shipwrecks (p.130). The third motif is of little village houses likened to ships at sea or at anchor: when he arrives at La Ferté-d'Angillon, he sees 'les maisons... toutes alignées au bord d'un fossé qui descendait la rue, comme autant de barques, voiles carguées, amarrées dans le calme du soir' (p.111); Meaulnes and Yvonne, alone together in their house after the wedding, are described by Seurel as 'comme deux passagers dans un bateau à la dérive' (p.136). Characters in the novel are several times likened to sailors: Seurel compares Meaulnes to the young Robinson Crusoe (p.13) and to a retired mariner, unable to break his lifelong practice of getting up from bed to keep the watches of the night. Meaulnes's imagination is no less haunted by phantoms from the sea. In the dining hall of *le domaine mystérieux*, he persuades himself on the not very convincing evidence of their being completely clean-shaven, that some of the elderly male guests must be retired sailors. Some of the characters do, in fact, have real associations with the sea — M. de Galais is a retired sea-captain, Meaulnes's uncle was once a marine, Frantz de Galais, who has been a naval cadet, makes his first appearance whistling a sea-shanty, and on his last appearance, is sporting 'une vieille casquette à ancre' (p.133) — but all the other intimations of the sea are imaginary, elements of the romantic vision of the beholder. The Cher *département* where Seurel grows up is as remote from the sea as it is possible to be in France, and to an untravelled, imaginative young person, it must possess an exotic emotional charge well beyond the ordinary. To invest everyday sights with maritime attributes, to see cottages as ships and peasants as sailors, is to create an atmosphere of mystery and excitement, to convey directly the sense of the 'other' landscape (see *12*, pp.234ff.; *13*, p.313; *24*, p.113 and *38*, pp.102-12).

Seurel's sense that the world he inhabits is strange and mysterious is reported at frequent intervals by his straightforward use of the adjectives 'étrange' and 'mystérieux' which occur in the narrative thirteen and seventeen times respectively (the examples are listed in *1*, pp.xc-xci). A key element in the mysteriousness is his ready response to suggestions of the vastness and emptiness of the countryside beyond his immediate horizons. The Sunday fishing his father regularly engages in is made to feel like an expedition to somewhere sinister and remote: 'mon père s'en allait au loin, sur le bord de quelque étang couvert de brume, pêcher le brochet dans une barque' (pp.4-5). After Meaulnes has disappeared without trace from the village school, Seurel hears 'l'appel lointain d'une bergère ou d'un gamin hélant son compagnon d'un bosquet de sapins à l'autre. Et chaque fois, ce long cri sur les coteaux déserts me faisait tressaillir, comme si c'eût été la voix de Meaulnes me conviant à le suivre au loin...' (p.18). He depicts Meaulnes on his way to *le château mystérieux*, riding ever further into 'la vaste campagne gelée, sans accident ni distraction aucune' (pp.28-29) until he is lost in the desolate heart of the Sologne:

'Pas un toit, pas une âme. Pas même le cri d'un courlis dans les roseaux des marais' (p.35). From the southern wing of the lost domain there is a vista of 'roseaux, à perte de vue, qui formaient tout le paysage' (p.48), while the older guests at *la fête étrange* are assumed to have undertaken lengthy journeys 'les uns, du fond de la campagne, les autres de villes lointaines' (p.43).

For Seurel, circumstances have decreed that he should lead a solitary, sedentary childhood. He is physically incapacitated. He is inhibited by an over-protective mother who is always aware of the family's superior social status and, partly because of her pride, partly because of the lack of suitable transport, journeys as far afield as Le Vieux-Nançay are a rare event. It is not, therefore, to be wondered at, that he should declare: 'Le Vieux-Nançay fut pendant très longtemps le lieu du monde que je préférais, le pays des fins de vacances' (p.104) and that 'à cette époque encore, je trouvais qu'il n'y avait de vraies vacances que passées en ce lieu' (p.105). Denied those opportunities of easy travel we nowadays take for granted, it is entirely in character that he should compensate for his enforced immobility through his roving imagination, and consistently feel that beyond the immediate horizon belongs to another world. To the romantic stay-at-home, the map takes on the features of a fable and, as D. Grojnowski has demonstrated in a convincingly argued article (*27*, pp.721-29), lanes, roads and highways are invested with rich romantic significance, leading either to some longed-for destination or on and away into the magical unknown.

His country world is mysterious to Seurel not only because he is so regularly reminded that it is vast and unexplored: it is also so often silent. The narrative is punctuated at remarkably frequent intervals with references to the stillness of characters or of the countryside, evoked by the noun 'silence', by adjectives or adverbs deriving therefrom, or by other words and phrases in the same semantic cluster (see *1*, p.xci).

On the impressionable Seurel, the silence of people has the same effect as the silence of the landscape. Habitual silence is a striking feature of Meaulnes's enigmatic personality: at moments of general schoolboy hilarity, 'il riait aussi, mais doucement, comme s'il eût réservé ses éclats de rire pour quelque meilleure histoire, connue de lui seul' (p.9). In like fashion, the unusually quiet countryside seems to be withholding some mysterious message like the fir-woods that line the horizon. When, in the course of the narrative, the stillness of the scene is broken, it is regularly in such a way as to accentuate that stillness and, at the same time, to point up the drama. Thus, Seurel, returning with his grandparents by pony and trap from the railway station, having seen no trace of Meaulnes:

> De temps à autre, sur le grand calme de l'après-midi gelé, montait l'appel lointain d'un gamin hélant son compagnon d'un bosquet de sapins à l'autre. Et chaque fois, ce long cri sur les coteaux déserts me faisait tressaillir, comme si c'eût été la voix de Meaulnes me conviant à le suivre au loin... (pp.17-18).

Thus, Meaulnes, driving through the lonely countryside at dusk, increasingly aware that he has lost his way: 'parfois une branche morte de la haie se prenait dans la roue et se cassait avec un bruit sec...' (p.30); thus, Frantz's owl-call piercing the stillness of the fir-woods surrounding the newly-weds' home (p.132), or the faint chiming of a distant bell, announcing that Yvonne is dying: 'Rien ne bougea. Pas une ombre suspecte; pas une branche qui remue. Mais, à la longue, là-bas, vers l'allée qui venait de Préveranges, j'entendis le son très fin d'une clochette...' (p.151).

Sometimes the pervasive silence is gently broken by the notes of a piano being played in the middle distance, evoking a mood of wistfulness in the listener. But the silence is, more often than not, broken by the sound of the wind, gusting and moaning through the gently undulating landscape as it does around the wildness of Wuthering Heights. As Alain-Fournier himself had to do when a child, Seurel has long been obliged to sleep alone, up above his parents' living quarters, in a dark and draughty attic, each night having to shield his guttering candle 'que menaçaient tous les courants d'air de la grande demeure' (p.23), frequently sensing that 'un vent noir et glacé soufflait dans le jardin mort et sur le toit' (p.25), and, as he tries to read in the fading light 'enfermé dans le cabinet des archives, plein de mouches mortes', always conscious of the 'affiches battant au vent' (p.9). Because of associations like these, the wind is consistently represented as a presence that is always unwelcome and sometimes distinctly sinister, presaging disaster or reminding revellers of harsh reality.

This helps create the impression of a sensitive, even animate Nature, able to influence and to be influenced by the moods and actions of the human characters. Before each of Frantz's disturbing entrances, an icy wind is blowing and rain is falling. When Seurel sets out, so full of confidence that he is about to rediscover the lost domain unaided, he feels that 'dans les champs et les bois, aux portes du bourg, commençait la plus radieuse matinée de printemps qui soit restée dans ma mémoire' (p.85); when his hopes are promptly dashed, the whole of Nature takes on a different aspect: 'Déjà ce n'était plus ce matin de printemps si frais et si luisant. Les bruits de l'après-midi avaient commencé. De loin en loin un coq criait, cri désolé! dans les fermes désertes aux alentours de la route' (p.89). The weather regularly seems to change to match the mood of the occasion, irrespective of the month of the year: when he first meets Yvonne in mid-December, 'Meaulnes se trouva comme transporté dans une journée de printemps' (p.47); when Meaulnes abruptly decides to leave Sainte-Agathe for Paris, although spring has come, Seurel notes that 'Toute la campagne était baignée dans une sorte de brume glacée comme aux plus mauvais jours de l'hiver' (p.91); at the end of *la partie de plaisir* which is staged in late August, 'le vent de cette fin d'été était si tiède sur le chemin des Sablonnières qu'on se serait cru au mois de mai, et les feuilles des haies tremblaient à la brise du sud...' (p.129); when Seurel arrives on a late September evening for his first sight of Yvonne's baby, 'Il faisait un soir si beau — un véritable soir d'été...' (p.149). Soon afterwards, Yvonne is dead, and Seurel rails at the sun for its treachery: 'Voilà donc ce que nous réservait ce beau matin de rentrée, ce perfide soleil d'automne qui glisse sous les branches' (p.152). This regular recourse to pathetic fallacy is essentially Romantic but in this un-Romantic narrative, Nature is rarely allowed to comfort or console. Seurel's world is characterized by a climate of extremes: the summer heat is always oppressive, the winter always icy, the rain always drenching. Just as his high hopes are forever being dashed, so the promise of the start of each day is consistently denied by evening.

The background sounds which accompany the unfolding drama are matched by 'lighting' effects, limited in their range but contributing significantly to the atmosphere. Again and again, for example, characters or scenes are set against a back-cloth of shadows or almost total darkness: Meaulnes first appears 'dans l'entrée obscure de la salle à manger' (p.7) and Seurel's first glimpses of him are 'dans la nuit tombante...', 'au préau, que l'obscurité envahissait déjà...' and 'à la lueur de la fin du jour...' (p.7); almost his final sight of him is near daybreak 'éclairé par le demi-jour' (p.189); before Meaulnes's arrival, one of Seurel's few lonely pleasures is to sit reading in the village mayor's gloomy office until he can no longer see and then, sitting on the lowest steps of the wooden staircase, watching his mother preparing the evening meal by the light of a guttering candle. Meaulnes's first glimpse of Frantz's aquiline profile is in a dark bedroom, by the flickering light of a candle (p.54), and when, finally, he recognizes him at Sainte-Agathe, it is in the light of a circus flare: 'On voyait, dans la lueur fumeuse, comme naguère à la lumière de la bougie, dans la chambre du Domaine, un très fin, très aquilin visage sans moustache'. When Seurel meets Yvonne for the very first time, he notes that 'la nuit commencait à tomber; une brume fraîche, plutôt de septembre que d'août, descendait avec la nuit' (p.107). After Yvonne has been deserted by Meaulnes, Seurel becomes her only friend and confidant: 'Souvent, je revins la voir. Souvent je causai avec elle auprès du feu, dans ce salon bas où la nuit venait plus vite que partout ailleurs' (p.141).

There are two other visual effects to which Seurel's imagination is especially responsive: shadowy shapes cast against a wall and dim light seen against surrounding darkness, through a closed or curtained window. An example of the first is Meaulnes's vast shadow, cast literally and metaphorically over Seurel's earliest memories of Sainte-Agathe. Examples of the second include one of his abiding childhood memories:

'Lorsqu'il faisait noir, que les chiens de la ferme voisine commençaient à hurler et que le carreau de notre petite cuisine s'illuminait, je rentrais enfin' (p.9). While Frantz is feverish and shut away inside the gipsy caravan, Meaulnes and Seurel loiter outside: 'Sur la place de l'église, le soir, nous allions rôder, rien que pour voir sa lampe derrière le rideau rouge de la voiture' (p.78). Seurel and Delouche mount a similar vigil, in a similar state of excited expectation, outside Meaulnes's cottage on his wedding-night: 'une lueur comme d'un feu allumé se reflète sur les carreaux de la fenêtre. De temps à autre, une ombre passe...' (p.131).

All of Seurel's 'special effects' — gathering gloom, light against dark, the voice of the wind as a sort of Chorus, and weather out of phase with the month of the year — are deployed in what is surely the strangest and most suggestive scene in the whole of the narrative. The episode is enacted 'par une soirée d'avril désolée comme une fin d'automne'. Meaulnes has long since departed in search of Frantz, and Seurel and Yvonne are out walking together. They are caught in a fierce hailstorm and lashed by an icy wind. They stand for a moment together 'pensifs, devant le paysage noirci. Je la revois, dans sa douce robe sévère, toute pâlie, toute tourmentée...' (p.142). She decides to visit the little house where Frantz used to play as a child, and when they arrive at the gate, Seurel fondly imagines that it is their own home to which they are returning: 'A voir Yvonne de Galais, on eût cru que cette maison nous appartenait et que nous l'avions abandonnée durant un long voyage' (ibid.). With the same anxiety that Seurel's mother displayed when inspecting the Sainte-Agathe schoolhouse on the occasion of the family's first arrival, Yvonne 'ouvrit, en se penchant, une petite grille, et se hâta d'inspecter avec inquiétude le lieu solitaire' (ibid.). The forsaken garden has been devastated by the storm which has left a nest of newly-born chicks dead or dying. Yvonne carefully deposits the survivors in a small bed, beneath a red silk eiderdown. Seurel stands beside her, 'et tandis qu'un rayon de soleil languissant, le premier et le dernier de la journée, faisait plus pâles nos visages et plus obscure la tombée de la nuit, nous étions là, debout, glacés et tourmentés, dans la maison étrange' (p.143). Every so often, Yvonne 'allait regarder dans le nid fiévreux, enlever un nouveau poussin mort pour l'empêcher de faire mourir les autres. Et chaque fois il nous semblait que quelque chose comme un grand vent par les carreaux cassés du grenier, comme un chagrin mystérieux d'enfants inconnus, se lamentait silencieusement'.

As in those clusters of images conveying Seurel's distinctly ambivalent reactions on Meaulnes's wedding-day, the writing in this episode is in a different mode altogether from that to be found in his uncomplicated and unambiguous impressions of village life. In this scene, everything and everywhere is confusion. If the sounds the couple 'seem' to hear are made not by the wind but by 'quelque chose *comme* le vent', what is making them? And how is the lamentation audible if it is being made *silencieusement*? And who is so desperately tormented over what? It would seem a quite extravagant display of emotion to be making over a few dead chicks, however pitiful the spectacle. Are Yvonne and Seurel grieving for the same reason? Yvonne's distress is easier to account for, indeed she readily explains that the little house and garden enshrine some of the most precious of her childhood memories. That Seurel should be quite so overcome, to be unable so speak, 'le cœur tout gonflé de sanglots...' (p.144) has to have a different cause: this is his very first visit to this particular place. Is this a coded message, I wonder, which Seurel cannot bring himself to decipher? Are the clues to its hidden meaning in the linguistic register of the descriptive detail which all has to do with maternal solicitude and the very young? Could those 'enfants inconnus' be the children Seurel knows that he and Yvonne will never have?

For the greater part of the narrative, Seurel expresses his feelings much less obscurely and much less obliquely. Sometimes the means he adopts are so direct as to seem old-fashioned, even naive by sophisticated standards. To stress the intensity of his emotional reaction, he will sometimes employ a straightforward expletive: 'qu'il faisait beau, mon Dieu!' (p.122). More commonly, he will simply combine a noun with one or two adjectives and, for good measure, add an exclamation mark: 'Etrange matinée! Etrange partie de plaisir!' (p.49); 'Amers souvenirs! Vains espoirs écrasés!' (p.84); 'Beau soir d'été calme!' (p.103); 'Triste fin de soirée!' (p.129); 'Epoque passée! Bonheur perdu!' (p.144): 'Précaires fiançailles!' (p.160). No less regularly, in the traditional manner of the teller of fairy-tales, he will use the superlative form of the adjective or a formulation with superlative effect: 'ce fut le matin le plus doux de cet hiver-là' (p.47); 'la plus radieuse matinée de printemps qui soit restée dans ma mémoire' (p.85). His very first sight of Yvonne, riding in an ancient family coach 'comme nous n'en avions jamais vu dans cette contrée', is recorded with studied artlessness: 'sur le siège — je le dis dans la simplicité de mon cœur, mais sachant bien ce que je dis — la jeune fille la plus belle qu'il y ait peut-être jamais eu au monde' (pp.108-09).

Seurel's parenthetical reference to the 'simplicité' of his heart is at once self-conscious and self-deceiving: in point of fact, as we have now had several occasions to observe, his heart is anything but simple. As often as not, his feelings are divided, and what causes him pain is frequently also a source of pleasure. His ambivalence is characteristically expressed through the juxtaposition of antithetical terms: 'les jours les plus tourmentés et les plus chers de ma vie' (p.3); 'une grande ombre inquiète et amie passe le long des murs' (p.4); 'je me glissais [au milieu des disputes] avec inquiétude et plaisir' (p.9); 'je me rappelle ce soir-là comme un des grands soirs de mon adolescence. C'était en moi un mélange de plaisir et d'anxiété' (p.12). He keeps his lonely vigil outside the house where, after Meaulnes's departure, Yvonne lives alone with her aged father 'heureux simplement d'être là, tout près de ce qui me passionnait et m'inquiétait le plus au monde' (p.146). The taste of bitter-sweetness is sharpest of all when he contemplates the impact Meaulnes had made on his life. Loneliness is replaced by companionship, a routine that is as placid as it is predictable is exchanged for the excitement of the unforeseeable, but Seurel is all too conscious of the price he has had to pay; near the very beginning of his narrative, he is moved to one of his rare flights of oratory:

Mais quelqu'un est venu qui m'a enlevé tous ces plaisirs d'enfant paisible. Quelqu'un a soufflé la bougie qui éclairait pour moi le doux visage maternel penché sur le repas du soir. Quelqu'un a éteint la lampe autour de laquelle nous étions une famille heureuse, à la nuit, lorsque mon père avait accroché les volets de bois aux portes vitrées. Et celui-là, ce fut Augustin Meaulnes... (p.9)

And he candidly voices his ambivalent sentiments when Meaulnes leaves the village school to pursue his quest in Paris:

Chose étrange: à cet ennui qui me désolait se mêlait comme une sensation de liberté. Meaulnes parti, toute cette aventure terminée et manquée, il semblait du moins que j'étais libéré de cet étrange souci, de cette occupation mystérieuse qui ne me permettaient plus d'agir comme tout le monde. Meaulnes parti, je n'étais plus son compagnon d'aventures, le frère de ce chasseur de pistes; je redevenais un gamin du bourg pareil aux autres. Et cela était facile et je n'avais qu'à suivre mon inclination la plus naturelle.

(p.93)

If the mixed feelings expressed here are entirely in character, so is the erroneous insistence that he is essentially a simple soul 'pareil aux autres'. As we have seen, this is the very opposite of the truth. From first to last, his emotional life is complex, increasingly so when Meaulnes marries the woman he himself has come to love and continues to worship, loyally but silently, throughout the period of Meaulnes's absence, until she dies, and forever after. Given that the weather is always so sensitive a reflector of Seurel's feelings, it is particularly appropriate that as Seurel first prepares to read Meaulnes's secret journal 'tantôt le soleil vif dessinait les croix des carreaux sur les rideaux blancs de la fenêtre, tantôt un vent brusque jetait aux vitres une averse glacée' (p.155). When, at the very end, Meaulnes returns at last to Les Sablonnières, Seurel's first sight of him does not generate instant joy: 'Un long moment je restai là, effrayé, désespéré, repris soudain par toute la douleur qu'avait réveillée son retour' (pp.170-71). Shortly afterwards, the baby daughter is reunited with her real father and Seurel reflects: 'La seule joie que m'eût laissée le grand Meaulnes, je sentais bien qu'il était revenu pour me la prendre' (p.171).

Throughout the instances of ambivalence we have just considered, the one common element is 'inquiétude', a state which, for Seurel, would seem to be congenital. At the very start of his narrative, he promptly attributes to his mother an ingrained condition of 'désespoir' (p.3), 'détresse' (p.4) and 'crainte' (p.6), and these, or sentiments like them, are a constant feature of his outlook. Anxious though his childhood and youth have been, they both have one quality which makes them infinitely precious to him: they are situated out of reach, in his past, in a world whose very remoteness makes it all the more desirable. The details he provides of his lost childhood nearly all evoke loneliness, discomfort, acute cold, and he will, on occasion, admit that he was 'un enfant malheureux et rêveur et fermé' (p.104), but when he calculates what Meaulnes's adventure has cost him, he mourns the loss of 'plaisirs d'enfant paisible', 'le doux visage maternel', 'la lampe autour de laquelle nous étions une famille heureuse' (p.9). When Meaulnes, in turn, seems to have disappeared forever from his life, he forgets the pain his presence regularly caused him and concentrates on the even greater pain caused by his absence. Back at Sainte-Agathe for the school holidays, he contemplates

> la grande cour sèche, le préau, la classe vide... Tout parlait du grand Meaulnes. Tout était rempli des souvenirs de notre adolescence déjà finie. Pendant ces longues journées jaunies, je m'enfermais comme jadis, avant la venue de Meaulnes, dans le cabinet des archives, dans les classes désertes. Je lisais, j'écrivais, je me souvenais... Mon père était à la pêche au loin. Millie dans le salon cousait ou jouait du piano comme jadis... Et dans le silence absolu de la classe... je pensais... que notre jeunesse était finie et le bonheur manqué... (pp.144-45)

When Yvonne dies soon after, he grieves not only for the loss of her but for a whole world of vanished values: 'Tout est pénible, tout est amer puisqu'elle est morte... Le monde est vide, les vacances sont finies. Finies les longues courses perdues en voiture; finie la fête mystérieuse...' (p.152).

To those afflicted with chronic nostalgia as Seurel, then is always preferable to now, and there to here. When, finally, after the impossible dreams of his youth have come true and he is allowed free access to what once seemed the irretrievably lost domain, just before actually taking up residence there, he is overwhelmed with yearning for the homely scenes of Sainte-Agathe and Le Vieux-Nançay: 'Tendrement, tristement, je rêvais aux chemins boueux de Sainte-Agathe, par ce même soir de septembre; j'imaginais la place pleine de brume, le garçon boucher qui siffle en allant à la pompe, le café illuminé, la joyeuse voiturée avec sa carapace de parapluies ouvertes qui arrivait avant la fin des vacances, chez l'oncle Florentin...' (p.146). The sights, sounds and scents of ordinary life are no less important to him than his memories of adventure and high romance. Belonging as they do to the past, they somehow seem more 'real'. If he retains undiminished fondness for the fontaine de Grand'Fons where he and his friends went for their summer picnics, it is because 'Il nous semblait, sur ces bords arides du Cher, que toute la fraîcheur terrestre était enclose en ce lieu. Et maintenant encore, au seul mot de fontaine, prononcé n'importe où, c'est à celle-là, pendant longtemps, que je pense' (p.102). Proust's Marcel treasures memories of his Combray childhood for the same reasons: 'soit que la foi qui crée soit tarie en moi, soit que la réalité ne se forme que dans la mémoire, les fleurs qu'on me montre aujourd'hui pour la première fois ne me semblent pas de vraies fleurs.'[2]

Unlike Proust's Marcel and unlike Meaulnes (see pp.84-85), Seurel is not allowed the consolations of involuntary memory, those chance coincidences between present and past sense-impressions which intimate, seemingly incontrovertibly, that the world we thought we had long lost still survives deep within us. For Seurel, Time's rule is inexorable, and whatever has gone, of good or ill, can never return. Tolling like a knell at intervals throughout his narrative are variations on the theme of 'never-

[2] *A la recherche du temps perdu* (Gallimard, Bibliothèque de la Pléiade, 1954), Vol.1, p.184.

more'. At the very outset, he states of the schoolhouse of Sainte-Agathe: 'la maison ne nous appartient plus... nous n'y reviendrons certainement jamais' (p.3); describing Meaulnes leaving his room at *le domaine mystérieux*, he refers to 'ce mystérieux endroit qu'il ne devait sans doute jamais revoir' (p.56); when, at the disastrous garden party, Meaulnes searches in vain for surviving relics of *la fête étrange*, Seurel instinctively feels they are 'ces beaux jours qui ne reviendraient plus' (p.127); recalling the months he spent as Yvonne's constant companion — 'Epoque passée! Bonheur perdu!' (p.144) — he grieves for 'tout un printemps et tout un été comme il n'y en aura jamais plus' (ibid.); and he describes Meaulnes's brooding over the fate to which he believes he has sentenced Valentine, and imagining her, at that moment, recounting memories of the childhood she spent in Bourges in a 'place morne où jamais elle ne viendrait plus' (p.167).

Unsubstantiated as it is by anything else in the narrative, this final comment, in which he is, in fact, speculating about another character's speculations about yet another character's thoughts and feelings, and clearly takes it as axiomatic that these are *bound to be* nostalgic — all this is wholly typical of Seurel. With his fondness for the half-lit and the shadowy, his abiding sense of deprivation and the deep wound to his psyche that seemingly will never heal, he could well say with Nerval's El Desdichado 'Je suis le Ténébreux — le Veuf — l'Inconsolé'. Like that eternally haunted figure, his one hope of consolation is through the agency of art. The detail of his vision and the accent of his voice testify that he has learnt the artist's bitter lesson that before he can begin to recreate his Paradise, he must first lose it utterly: from that feeling of total loss emerges the urge to restore, the need for revenge over circumstance and for victory over Time.

4. The Characters and their Relationships

Seurel is not merely a chronicler of events; he is a dramatized character closely involved with the other characters and he plays an increasingly influential role in the action. His judgments of the people around him, like his view of scenery and situations, is invariably subjective and sometimes suspect; this is even more apposite of statements he makes, from time to time, about himself and of the 'explanations' he provides to account for the activities of Meaulnes.

As if to dramatize the contrast between the life he leads after Meaulnes's arrival and the life he had led previously, he stresses how lonely he used to be. The schoolhouse stands isolated from the rest of the village (p.5), his mother insists on his keeping aloof from his local peer-group for what seem to be snobbish reasons, he is physically incapacitated by his hip-affliction and his parents are so preoccupied with being busy that he appears permanently to have been left to his own devices. At the outset, he seems to be solitary, anxious, timorous, somewhat over-protected, and, at intervals throughout his narrative, he reminds us of his immaturity: when Meaulnes waxes indignant over the schoolboys who have deserted him for Frantz, the fifteen-year-old Seurel comments 'enfant paisible que j'étais, je ne manquais pas de l'approuver' (p.70); when Meaulnes, Frantz and Seurel make their solemn pact, he explains 'nous jurâmes, car, enfants que nous étions, tout ce qui était plus solennel et plus sérieux que nature nous séduisait' (p.75); when his mother decides to dry the family washing indoors, he declares 'au premier instant — j'étais si jeune encore! — je considérai cette nouveauté comme une fête' (p.91); when he decides to mount guard outside the house of his newly-married best friends, he reflects 'Ils sont heureux enfin. Meaulnes est là-bas près d'elle... Et savoir cela, en être sûr, suffit au contentement parfait du brave enfant que je suis' (p.132) — an assertion subverted by the cluster of enigmatic images with which he reacts to the occasion (see above, pp.29-31); of his feelings for Yvonne, he states 'je la regardai et j'étais content, comme un petit enfant' (p.152).

This tactic of stressing the fact that he is 'petit' is complemented by another emphasizing that Meaulnes is 'grand'; the adjective is so consistently applied that it has become virtually an integral part of the character's name, and the policy of building him up while he plays himself down is put into effect from the very outset. Even before Seurel is impressed by the dramatic coincidence of Meaulnes's arrival and the sudden curing of his own chronic coxalgia, which makes him think of his new-found friend as a species of miracle-worker, the campaign of hero-worship is already under way. Before Meaulnes has appeared on the scene at all, Seurel is 'intrigued' by Madame Meaulnes's 'air supérieur et mystérieux' (p.6) when describing him. His reaction to her remarks seems quite extravagant: Meaulnes is said to wander for miles beside lonely river-banks, to return with wild birds' eggs, to spread the occasional net and, recently, to have come across a pheasant. These are not, one would think, particularly remarkable incidents in the life of a seventeen-year-old youth living in the heart of the countryside. Seurel's class-mates engage in activities that are not dramatically dissimilar, but he nonetheless describes Madame Meaulnes's account as 'fort surprenant' and listens 'avec étonnement' (p.6). When he first arrived at Sainte-Agathe, Seurel, then a very young child wearing a 'grand chapeau de paille à rubans', stayed timorously in the school playground 'à attendre, à fureter petitement autour du puits et sous le hangar' (p.4); when Meaulnes first arrives, the seventeen-year-old promptly deserts his mother, goes up uninvited into the school attics, comes down with an unexploded Catherine wheel, is seen to be 'un grand garçon' sporting 'un chapeau de feutre paysan', pointedly ignores the adults, marches Seurel out into the dark playground and produces a box of matches 'à mon grand étonnement, car cela nous était formellement interdit' (p.8). All this while, Seurel's mother, normally so insistently censorious and protective, remains uncharacteristically silent. It is by no means impossible that, in the presence of a prospective pupil's parent,

she is simply being polite, but Seurel will have none of this: 'elle
n'osa rien dire' (p.8), she too is presumed to be under
Meaulnes's spell and her despotic reign at last seems to be over.
For Seurel, it is Meaulnes who now rules but, as I shall presently
hope to demonstrate, not for long: Seurel will come to dominate
the action just as he rules the narrative. He will, before either of
them is much older, begin to dominate Meaulnes, though all the
while, making him worthy of his hero-worship, by glamorizing
him. To make a thorough job of this, he draws on the literary
heritage of his own lonely childhood.

Seurel's major source of consolation as a solitary, sedentary
child, has been his reading: regularly, on Sundays, for example,
'les vêpres finies, j'attendais, en lisant dans la froide salle à
manger' (p.5) and, indeed, every day, after school, when the
other pupils go out to play 'tant qu'il y avait une lueur de jour...
je lisais...' (p.9). What he reads so assiduously is never specified:
one assumes it is likely to be an unexceptional staple diet of
fables, precautionary tales, *livres de prix*, and adventure stories.
Certainly, by the time Meaulnes has arrived, he is well versed in
Defoe because, as he observes Meaulnes meditating in the village
blacksmith's shop, he recalls a not particularly familiar passage
explaining where Crusoe acquired his knowledge of basket-
weaving: 'je pensai soudain à cette image de *Robinson Crusoé*,
où l'on voit l'adolescent anglais, avant son grand départ,
fréquentant la boutique d'un vannier...' (p.13). To Seurel,
Meaulnes is a very special sort of hero: he is like a hero out of a
book, and once this notion is planted in his imagination, it
proves impossible to eradicate. Before Meaulnes had divulged
what happened to him during his three days of mysterious
absence from school, Seurel speculates: 'C'est à une jeune fille
certainement qu'il pensait la nuit, comme un héros de roman'
(pp.26-27). When Meaulnes looks at his reflection in the pool at
le domaine mystérieux, Seurel reports (or possibly glosses?), 'il
crut voir un autre Meaulnes... un être charmant et romanesque,
au milieu d'un beau livre de prix...' (p.47). When he sets out
himself, hoping to find the lost domain, Seurel announces that
his quest is for something more fabulous than 'cette fontaine
profonde et tarie, couverte d'un grillage, enfouie sous tant

d'herbes folles qu'il fallait chaque fois plus de temps pour la retrouver… Je cherche quelque chose de plus mystérieux encore. C'est le passage dont il est question dans les livres, l'ancien chemin obstrué, celui dont le prince harassé de fatigue n'a pu trouver l'entrée' (p.88): as like as not, he is thinking here of *The Sleeping Beauty*. For him, what makes the escapades of Meaulnes so gratifying is that they are like a book made real or, even more exciting, like real life transformed into a book. Ostensibly, he is narrating events that are supposed actually to have happened: we, as readers, naturally know that we are listening to a fiction but the contract we have made with this particular narrator is that he pretends, and we pretend, it is all *real*. That contract seems to have been blatantly breached when Seurel describes Meaulnes as 'notre voyageur' (p.32) and 'notre héros' (p.42) and when, after reading the third and most despairing of Meaulnes's three letters from Paris, he concludes 'En février, pour la première fois de l'hiver, la neige tomba, ensevelissant définitivement notre roman d'aventures' (p.99). The two key-terms here, 'aventures' and 'roman', need to be considered more closely.

The word 'aventure' and its derivatives sound like a refrain throughout the whole length of the narrative. It is first heard very near the outset when the village school is likened to some lonely rock over which ebb and flow and break like waves '*nos aventures*' (so timorous, stay-at-home Seurel has already anticipated the sea-change to his temperament!). The final sentence of the novel shows Seurel, unrepentantly Romantic to the last; Meaulnes has only just been reunited with his baby daughter at daybreak when Seurel comments 'Et déjà je l'imaginais, la nuit, enveloppant sa fille dans un manteau, et partant avec elle pour de nouvelles aventures' (p.171). Even although Alain-Fournier has not italicized the main verb, and it could, surely, hardly be clearer that this dramatic departure is taking place in Seurel's imagination, eminent critics seem to accept without question that Meaulnes departs in just this fashion. Léon Cellier, for example, in a short study almost wholly hostile to *Le Grand Meaulnes*, likens Meaulnes's alleged mode of departure to a thief's making off with the swag: 'Que dire de cette ultime évasion? Meaulnes nous apparaît condamné à une fuite éternelle. Et c'est ainsi qu'à l'image mythique du chevalier errant se substitue celle du fratricide errant. Caïn, qu'as-tu fait de ton frère? Le roman de l'initiation aboutit à un absurde roman de remords' (*23*, p.25). This seems to me a perverse mis-representation of Meaulnes's actions and motives, but the critic is not entirely to blame: I think he has been deceived by Seurel's insidiously romantic rhetoric.

Between the first and last references to 'aventures' there are no fewer than twenty-eight others. Seurel uses the term so regularly and so instinctively that it becomes as inseparable from the character of Meaulnes as the adjective 'grand'. Initially, and not inappropriately, it serves to designate everything that happens to him between his driving away from school, standing up arrogantly on Fromentin's farm-cart, 'comme un conducteur de char romain' (p.15), as Seurel puts it, and returning three days later, 'la tête haute et comme ébloui', looking like a 'voyageur fatigué, affamé mais émerveillé' (p.20). Quite understandably, Seurel is entranced: Meaulnes has behaved completely in character. Ever since M. Seurel passed him over for Mouchebœuf to ride with François to meet the grand-parents, he has been expecting of him 'quelque entreprise extra-ordinaire qui vînt tout bouleverser' (p.12). Seurel's immediate response at the sight of Meaulnes returning is entirely in character too: 'Je me rappelle combien je le trouvai beau à cet instant, le grand compagnon, malgré son air épuisé et ses yeux rougis par les nuits passées au dehors, sans doute' (p.20). And it is both credible and consistent that, on hearing the full story of Meaulnes's experiences, his adulation should increase immeasurably and that those experiences should regularly be described as 'sa bizarre aventure' (p.32), 'l'étrange aventure' (p.39) 'la belle aventure' (p.126) or 'l'aventure manquée' (p.93). What is rather less justifiable is Seurel's assumption that Meaulnes, the runaway schoolboy and uninvited guest at *la fête étrange*, has 'un cœur aventureux' (p.141) and has made common cause with 'les solitaires, les chasseurs et les hommes d'aventures' (pp.117-18). Is this really so?

Certainly Meaulnes is wilful and impulsive and not entirely

devoid of arrogance. It is pique at having been slighted by M. Seurel which prompts him to borrow the horse and cart and ride off on his own, but his objectives are both specific and domestic. He certainly does not conform with O. Henry's concept of 'the true adventurer' who 'goes forth aimless and uncalculating to meet and greet unknown fate' (*The Green Door*): he genuinely intends to drive to the railway station, pick up Seurel's grand-parents and bring them back to the village school. Far from being dashing, determined, intrepid, bold or resolute, as he rides along his way he becomes progressively more anxious (p.29) and, as darkness falls, Seurel reports that 'Meaulnes songea soudain, avec un serrement de cœur, à la salle à manger à Sainte-Agathe' (p.30). When he discovers that his horse has wandered off, he feels 'en proie à ce désir panique qui ressemblait à la peur' (p.33), and when, eventually, he takes refuge for the night in the shepherd's hut, 'il se sentit si malheureux, si fâché contre lui-même qu'il lui prit une forte envie de pleurer' (p.34). Once he has wandered into *la fête étrange*, he displays none of the cock-sureness which characterized his very first appearance at Sainte-Agathe: all the time, he is indecisive, nervous and anxious, aware that he is an uninvited guest and fearful of being denounced. If he is like a hero from one of Seurel's books, then it clearly is not a tale of derring-do. By the same token, the prospects which most stir his imagination are not of hazardous enterprises, of trails being blazed or of perils confronted and overcome. They are the very epitome of domesticity: his most precious dream, which he recalls the night before he arrives at *le domaine mystérieux*, is of waking up to find his young wife in the room beside him, quietly sewing beside a window; it seems to have come true both at *la fête étrange*, when he sits quietly, surrounded by small children, listening to a young lady playing her piano and, much later, when he spends a week-end in the country with Valentine. If he grows increasingly frenetic at the Sainte-Agathe school and departs abruptly for Paris, it is not because of congenital wanderlust. And if he briefly con-templates breaking into Yvonne's Paris home to look for the location of the lost domain, it is not because of the adventurer's love of risk. It is because he is desperate to rediscover Yvonne, marry her and lead a peaceful married life. If, having been unexpectedly reunited with her, he abruptly deserts her the day after the wedding, it is not for the reasons that Seurel suggests to Yvonne: 'Tant de folies dans une si noble tête! Peut-être le goût des aventures plus fort que tout...' (p.147). Although Yvonne dismisses these notions for the nonsense we know them to be, and although Seurel subsequently discovers the real reason — Meaulnes's compulsive urge to cleanse his conscience by 'saving' Valentine — he persists to the very end in thinking of Meaulnes as an 'adventurer'. The first English translator of *Le Grand Meaulnes* was clearly misled by Seurel's special pleading when she entitled her book *The Wanderer* (translated by Françoise Deslisle, Paul Elek, 1928) and compounded the felony by speaking of the eponymous hero as 'Admiral' Meaulnes throughout! If Meaulnes does wander, it is because of circumstances rather than temperament. The object of his restless movement is domestic stasis; he travels not 'for lust of knowing what should not be known' but simply in search of wife and home.

In arguing that Meaulnes is rather less 'adventurous' than the narrator would have us to believe, I do not not mean to suggest that he is merely an enlarged mirror-image of Seurel himself, physically more robust, but with all of his doubts, fears and inhibitions. The overwhelming attraction Seurel feels for him is, in part, gratitude for ending his own loneliness and physical incapacity, but, in larger measure, it is the attraction of opposites: Meaulnes is admired when Seurel is despised or, at best, patronized; Meaulnes is free to roam beyond the horizons in which Seurel is confined; Meaulnes will take decisive action while Seurel will merely yearn. This characterizes their relationship at the outset but, significantly, in the course of time, each seems influenced by the attitude of the other. After his return from *la fête étrange*, Meaulnes appears much less decisive: on three separate occasions (pp.25, 27 and 78-79), the cautious Seurel persuades his 'adventurous' companion not to set out in search of the lost domain until the return of milder days and shorter nights. More to the point, he exacts from Meaulnes a solemn promise that the two of them will set out together.

Meaulnes's 'adventure' becomes Seurel's 'adventure' too. What he first describes as 'son étrange aventure' (p.28) or, with a rhetorical flourish, 'ses aventures' (p.34) soon becomes 'nos aventures', 'toute notre aventure' (p.154) or even 'notre roman d'aventures' (p.99). After the death of Yvonne he can go so far as to say: 'Nous avions retrouvé la belle jeune fille. Nous l'avions conquise' (p.152), the most significant of all the expressions of his possessive sense of involvement.

Seurel's great opportunity for positive involvement comes with Delouche's disclosure of the name and whereabouts of the lost domain. There and then, he resolves to intervene, and, as if by magic, his new-found decisiveness brings new-found physical strength: 'je devins résolu et, comme on dit chez nous, "décidé" lorsque je sentis que dépendait de moi l'issue de cette grave aventure. Ce fut, je crois bien, à dater de ce soir-là que mon genou cessa définitivement de me faire mal' (p.104). When he confronts Meaulnes with the good news, it is his friend who seems to lack self-confidence and Seurel who dominates:

> Il paraissait complètement désemparé et continuait à ne rien répondre.
>
> Il faut tout de suite décommander ton voyage, dis-je avec impatience. Allons avertir ta mère...
>
> Et comme nous descendions tous les deux:
>
> Cette partie de campagne?... me demanda-t-il avec hésitation. Alors, vraiment, il faut que j'y aille?...
>
> —Mais, voyons, répliquai-je, cela ne se demande pas.
>
> Il avait l'air de quelqu'un qu'on pousse par les épaules.
>
> (p.120)

What Seurel does not know at this juncture is the story of Meaulnes's involvement with Valentine. What Meaulnes does not know is that Seurel has just learnt Valentine's Paris address and that he can readily find her for him. The continuing silence of both on these matters is to have momentous consequences. The American critic, Ruth Gross, finds Seurel's manipulation of events so emphatic she insists that he comes to exercise truly demonic power over events and the narrative (*28*); Martin

Sorrell argues that Seurel deeply resents Meaulnes and that both his actions and his structuring of the narrative in Part III express a desire to be a hero on his own particular terms (*34*, pp.79-87). Both of these fail to make what seems to me an important paradoxical point. This is that while Alain-Fournier is trying, first and foremost, to write a novel like life, Seurel, as we have seen, feels he is living his life like a novel. To judge by his miscalculations, that novel is of an old-fashioned species, in which hero and heroine fall in love at first sight, are separated through circumstances, but are finally reunited, marry and live happily ever after. This sentimental scenario which he hopes he can stage-manage, does not allow for disturbing departures like the hero becoming engaged to the fiancée of his beloved's brother, or the story-teller himself being in love with both of his best friends. But this is the real-life novel in which Seurel becomes enmeshed and it is one for which his previous reading seems to have left him ill-prepared: he should — like Alain-Fournier himself — have progressed from Defoe to Dostoevsky.

About the innermost feelings of the central characters, we are singularly ill-informed. We are rarely directly in touch with them and our knowledge of them derives, for the most part, from descriptions by Seurel or from the occasional short speech or sign. So, we infer the depth of Yvonne's feelings for Meaulnes by her spontaneous reaction to the sudden discovery that Seurel is his friend: 'Mlle de Galais s'était levée, soudain devenue très pâle. Et, à ce moment précis, je me rappelai que Meaulnes, autrefois, dans le Domaine singulier, près de l'étang, lui avait dit son nom...' (p.110). Similarly, when Seurel announces to Meaulnes that the domain and the still unmarried Yvonne have both been found, 'Il me regarda, puis, détournant brusquement les yeux, rougit comme je n'ai jamais vu quelqu'un rougir: une montée de sang qui devait lui cogner à grands coups dans les tempes...', while a few moments later, 'il était maintenant affreusement pâle' (p.119). In conversation either with Seurel or with each other, both Meaulnes and Yvonne are relatively reserved. Meaulnes may engage in extravagant physical action but the verbal expressions of his feelings for Yvonne are — compared with Seurel's displays of rhetoric — decidedly discreet: the three letters he sends from Paris tell us more about the world around him than the world within. We are rather better informed about his feelings for Valentine, even although the diary which provides that information has been carefully 'edited' by Seurel. We learn, for example, that the relationship is no mere *passade*, that, for all their temperamental difficulties, the couple have much in common, and that, at least, on one occasion, Valentine comes remarkably close to fulfilling Meaulnes's lifelong ideal.

On the eve of his arrival at *le domaine mystérieux*, Meaulnes

> se rappela un rêve — une vision plutôt, qu'il avait eue tout enfant, et dont il n'avait jamais parlé à personne: un matin, au lieu de s'éveiller dans sa chambre, où pendaient ses culottes et ses paletots, il s'était trouvé dans une longue pièce verte, aux tentures pareilles à des feuillages. En ce lieu coulait une lumière si douce qu'on eût cru pouvoir la goûter. Près de la première fenêtre, une jeune fille cousait, le dos tourné, semblant attendre son réveil... Il n'avait pas eu la force de se glisser hors de son lit pour marcher dans cette demeure enchantée. Il s'était rendormi... Mais la prochaine fois, il jurait bien de se lever... Demain matin, peut-être!... (p.35)

The following evening, at *la fête étrange*, he sits in a candle-lit room, with a small child on each knee, listening to a piano being played in the neighbouring room. Seurel comments 'ce fut un rêve comme son rêve de jadis' (p.46), though the resemblance between the scene at the *fête* and the childhood dream or vision seems fairly remote: there is an unknown young lady in each, but what she is doing, and where and when she is doing it, are quite different in each scene, as are the position and the immediate surroundings of Meaulnes. On the other hand, when he spends a week-end with Valentine, at a farmhouse in June, we learn:

> Lorsqu'il s'éveilla de grand matin dans la chambre de l'auberge, le soleil avait allumé les dessins rouges du rideau

noir. Des ouvriers agricoles, dans la salle du bas, parlaient
fort... Depuis longtemps sans doute Meaulnes entendait,
dans son sommeil, ce calme bruit. Car il n'y prit point
garde d'abord. Ce rideau semé de grappes rougies par le
soleil, ces voix matinales montaient dans la chambre
silencieuse, tout cela se confondait dans l'impression
unique d'un réveil à la campagne, au début de délicieuses
grandes vacances.

Il se leva, frappa doucement à la porte voisine, sans
obtenir de réponse, et l'entrouvrit sans bruit. Il aperçut
alors Valentine et comprit d'où lui venait tant de paisible
bonheur. Elle dormait, absolument immobile et
silencieuse, sans qu'on l'entendît respirer, comme un
oiseau doit dormir. Longtemps il regarda ce visage
d'enfant aux yeux fermés, et visage si quiet qu'on eût
souhaité ne l'éveiller et ne le troubler jamais...' (p.161)

On this occasion, Seurel does not draw the parallel with the
childhood 'vision' as he does when presenting the piano episode
at *la fête étrange*, but he could well have done: Valentine is
discovered asleep rather than sewing beside a window, otherwise
the various details concerning time of day, décor of curtains or
drapery that looks like foliage, Meaulnes rising from sleep and
experiencing blissful euphoria at the scene before him — all have
a great deal in common. The one observation made about all
these proceedings, after Valentine has got up, tidied the room
and taken a knife to scrape some mud caked on the lower leg of
Meaulnes's trousers, is: 'telle était bien la compagne que devait
souhaiter, avant son aventure mystérieuse, le chasseur et le
paysan qu'était le grand Meaulnes' (p.161); this reads like a
comment by Seurel rather than a paraphrase of anything
scribbled, in this allegedly illegible section of the diary, by
Meaulnes. His innermost thoughts here, as elsewhere, are kept
well concealed.

He affects not to be able to remember his exact reply when
Valentine asked if he wanted to marry her: 'J'ai balbutié. Je ne
sais pas ce que j'ai répondu. Peut-être ai-je dit: Oui' (p.160),
evasiveness which might be comprehensible were he speaking

with some embarrassment to a third party, but which serves little purpose as an entry in a diary meant for no eyes other than his own. On the other hand, he can recall all too clearly how he reacted on learning from Valentine that she was once engaged to Frantz de Galais: 'C'était mon ami le meilleur, c'était mon frère d'aventures, et voilà que je lui ai pris sa fiancée!' (p.164). And he can recall Valentine's equally melodramatic response: 'Je rentrerai à Bourges, chez nous, avec ma sœur. Et si vous ne revenez pas me chercher, vous savez, n'est-ce pas? que mon père est trop pauvre pour me garder; eh bien, je repartirai pour Paris, je battrai les chemins comme je l'ai déjà fait une fois, je deviendrai certainement une fille perdue, moi qui n'ai plus de métier' (p.164). The couple separate in mid-June, Meaulnes goes through 'une période de combats affreux et misérables, dans un isolement absolu', until, on 25 August, he returns to Bourges to seek a reconciliation; Valentine has departed for Paris, leaving her mother instructions that whilst her new address is not to be divulged, letters will be forwarded from the old one known to Meaulnes. Yvonne de Galais, he believes, is long since married, and it is not of her he is thinking when Seurel comments: 'pour Meaulnes, à ce moment, il n'existait plus qu'un seul amour, cet amour mal satisfait qu'on venait de souffleter si cruellement, et la jeune fille entre toutes qu'il eût dû protéger, sauvegarder, était justement celle-là qu'il venait d'envoyer à sa perte' (p.167). Towards the end of this same month of August, Seurel discovers the whereabouts of Les Sablonnières and that Yvonne is not married after all. Uncle Florentin arranges his garden-party for the following week and, that same evening, Meaulnes proposes to Yvonne. Thereafter, his feelings about Valentine remain a mystery. To judge by the eloquent silence about them in the narrative thereafter, he ceases to speak about such serious matters to Seurel.

Meaulnes's feelings about Seurel are never disclosed either but it seems more than likely that he does not reciprocate the intense adulation with which Seurel at all times regards him. The feelings he professes to have for Frantz seem remarkably ill-founded, given that for more than half of the time he has hitherto spent in close proximity to him, the two regarded each other as mortal enemies, and that, out of what looks very much like gratuitous spite, Frantz pretends not to know the whereabouts of his own home. The extravagant eulogy of him that he delivers to Valentine may well be a reflex act of retaliation, to shock her as much as her revelation has just shocked him, but in reacting so theatrically at mention of his name, he is in the best of company: Yvonne is heart-broken 'd'avoir perdu son frère si fou, si charmant et si admiré' (p.143); his parents are happy to indulge him like a medieval princeling, giving him his own little house in the woods when he is just a few years old; Seurel remains lukewarm about his antics, finding 'cet enfantillage pénible à supporter chez ce garçon déjà légèrement vieilli' and deprecating 'ce rôle absurde de jeune héros romantique où je le voyais s'entêter' (p.135), but he, in turn is inspired by Frantz's presence to fix a rendezvous with him in conventionally Romantic terms, 'dans un an exactement, à cette même heure' (ibid.), just as, earlier, he had unhesitatingly responded to Frantz's pressing demand that the three of them should solemnly swear forever to be allies: 'et nous jurâmes, car, enfants que nous étions, tout ce qui était plus solennel et plus sérieux que nature nous séduisait' (p.75).

If Seurel's insistence that they are still children is very much in character (though, at this juncture, both Meaulnes and Frantz are actively seeking to marry the girls they love), so also are both the form and content of Frantz's demand. Frantz's true vocation is clearly that of impresario. He is an inspired designer of colourful spectacle with an irrepressible urge to create *coups de théâtre*. His imagination seems to have been as coloured by Hugo's *Hernani* as Seurel's by *Robinson Crusoe*. *La fête étrange* — with the mixture of guests young and old, and the fairy-lighting and entertainments — was all designed by him, as Valentine explains: 'Voici ce que me promettait mon fiancé, comme un enfant qu'il était: tout de suite nous aurions eu une maison, comme une chaumière perdue dans la campagne. Elle était toute prête... Nous y serions arrivés comme au retour d'un grand voyage, le soir de notre mariage, vers cette heure-ci qui est proche de la nuit. Et par les chemins, cachés dans les bosquets, des enfants inconnus nous auraient fait fête, criant: ''Vive la

mariée!'''' (p.163). The nocturnal raid he leads on the schoolhouse at Sainte-Agathe, and the ambush into which he lures
Meaulnes in order to steal the partially completed map, fill him
with particular pleasure: 'Vous avez vu cet abordage, hier au
soir, comme c'était conduit, comme ça marchait! Depuis mon
enfance, je n'avais rien organisé d'aussi réussi' (p.74). It seems a
waste of his undoubted talents to be touring remote villages in
the company of Ganache in order to stage their 'pantomimes...
chansons... fantaisies équestres...' (p.79), though he shows he
has not lost his touch, or his timing, when he removes the
bandage from his head to reveal his true identity, at the very end
of the Sainte-Agathe performance, and when he arrives, very
much on cue, to deliver his owl-call signal on the day of
Meaulnes's marriage.

   His theatrical 'performances' are matched with a capacity for
flamboyant utterance. Having brought *la fête étrange* into
being, he decrees that it should abruptly end, dismisses
Meaulnes with an imperious 'Qu'on ne me dérange pas!' (p.54),
writes what amounts to a suicide note, and tries to blow his
brains out. When he enrols as a very temporary pupil at Sainte-
Agathe, and the collection of knick-knacks he has brought to
impress the village boys has ended up on Meaulnes's desk, the
nonplussed Monsieur Seurel asks who it belongs to: Frantz
replies '''C'est à moi''... Et il ajouta aussitôt, avec un geste large
et élégant de jeune seigneur auquel le vieux instituteur ne sut pas
résister: ''Mais je les mets à votre disposition, monsieur, si vous
voulez regarder''' (pp.68-69). In much more truculent mood,
addressing Seurel in the dark wood outside the house of the
newly married Meaulnes, he declares, 'repris par sa terrible
puérilité: ''Appelez votre Delouche... parce que si je le
rencontrais ce serait affreux''' (p.135). Several of his utterances
on this occasion are so extravagant that one wonders if he has
taken leave of his senses. He declares that he and Ganache have
spent three years searching the length and breadth of France for
Valentine, when a conversation with her parents in Bourges
(where they first met) would surely have put him on her track.
He claims to have left their caravan far away, and to have undertaken a non-stop thirty-hour route-march to get to Les

Sablonnières to prevent the wedding. The alleged motive is to persuade Meaulnes to help him look for Valentine, 'comme il a cherché le Domaine des Sablonnières' (p.135), omitting to mention that Meaulnes completely failed to find the Domain, and failed because Frantz refused to show him the way. He announces 'Nous serons dans trois jours sur les routes d'Allemagne', not the most likely place, one would have thought, to look for a seamstress from Bourges. One can only assume that this is yet another theatrical flourish, Frantz's personal equivalent of 'We take the Golden Road to Samarkand'.

Unlike Meaulnes and Yvonne, Seurel is able to see Frantz for the meretricious mountebank he essentially is, doubtless because he is fundamentally hostile to him. The two are directly antithetical in several important ways: the name 'Frantz' is the exotic, Teutonic version of the homely, French 'François'; he is a flamboyant extrovert while Seurel is a diffident brooder; his influence and example are forever tempting Meaulnes to depart while Seurel's instinct consistently prompts him to stay; because he has the inestimable distinction of being part of the charmed world of *le domaine mystérieux*, Frantz is seen by Seurel as a threatening rival for Meaulnes's affection. Unsympathetic though he is to Frantz, even Seurel has to concede that 'naguère, il y avait en lui tant d'orgueilleuse jeunesse que toute folie au monde lui paraissait permise' (pp.134-35) — charm which is never properly realized within the novel and which we, as readers, have to take on trust. Significantly — and somewhat paradoxically — it is Seurel, with his profound attachment to childhood — who sternly insists: 'Voyons, Frantz... le temps des fantasmagories et des enfantillages est passé' (p.134) and observes 'cet enfantillage était pénible à supporter chez ce garçon déjà légèrement vieilli...' (ibid.). And, no less paradoxically, it is Seurel, who so admires the 'adventurous' spirit of Meaulnes, who says of Frantz: 'A présent, on était d'abord tenté de le plaindre pour n'avoir pas réussi sa vie; puis de lui reprocher ce rôle absurde de jeune héros romantique où je le voyais s'entêter...' (p.135).

The hardening of Seurel's attitude towards Frantz needs to be

contrasted with a corresponding softening of his attitude
towards Jasmin Delouche. At the outset, this character is presented in decidedly pejorative terms: 'Il avait une figure pâle,
assez fade, et les cheveux pommadés' (p.22). The whole of his
Christian name seems redolent of the lotion used to plaster down
his hair, the second half of his surname to be indicative of his
preoccupation with the pub-talk of the village men and the love-
life of the village girls. When Frantz declares: 'C'est ce Delouche
surtout qui me déplaît. Quelle idée de faire l'homme à dix-sept
ans! Rien de me dégoûte davantage...' (p.74), the absence of
comment from the narrator conveys his assent, though the
attentive reader will have observed that Frantz himself was a
householder before he was ten, and was seeking to marry
Valentine when he was fifteen years old. Delouche continues to
be viewed in a hostile light during the entertainment staged by
Frantz and Ganache in the village square — 'Il se tenait les
pouces au revers de son veston, dans une attitude à la fois très
fate et très gênée' (p.80) — while his action of denouncing them
to the gendarmes for raiding the local chicken-coops is
represented as somehow being bad form. Thereafter, through a
number of slight but suggestive touches, he ceases to be the
villain of the piece. Seurel refers to him more and more
frequently by his Christian name and makes him progressively
more agreeable. When Meaulnes refers obliquely to the journey
which led him to the lost domain, Delouche shows friendly
interest and concern, 'comme s'il eût été lui-même un peu dans
le secret' (p.91); Meaulnes pointedly ignores him. One of the
novel's several ironies, of course, is that Delouche is indeed
'dans le secret', and that had Meaulnes been less boorish than he
habitually is with Delouche, he would have found the lost
domain so much sooner. When, months later, Delouche
reappears in the narrative, he does not seem to have mended his
juvenile ways. He still finds it daring to smoke cigarettes, to
shout mild insults at the occasional passing nun from behind a
convenient hedge, or to pass on risqué gossip about Gilberte
Poquelin, the 'fastest' girl in the village, but now Seurel is very
much more indulgent: 'Mais enfin le cas n'est pas encore
désespéré...' (p.100), is his comment, and Delouche goes on to

become a useful citizen and a loyal friend both to Seurel and to the de Galais family. He does not really change; he remains, as he always has been, 'un gamin du bourg pareil aux autres'. The change is in Seurel: his acceptance of Delouche and his rejection of Frantz de Galais demonstrate that he has, after much travail, come of age.

None of which should be taken to mean that he ever really ceases to attach very particular importance to the world of childhood. We have seen (p.57 above), how frequently Seurel ascribes childlike qualities to himself. Similar references are made, if less frequently, to all the other main characters: Meaulnes (p.59), Yvonne de Galais (pp.57, 139), Frantz (pp.54, 83, 135) and Valentine (p.161); even the twenty-year-old Delouche, with his disturbing grown-up proclivities, is described as 'le vieux petit gars' (p.100). 'Enfantin' or 'comme un enfant' are, in Seurel's vocabulary, compliments or terms of endearment. Their antonyms are 'puéril' or 'enfantillage'. The distinction between these two sets of antithetical terms is a rather nice one, as fine as that between Meaulnes's 'aventures' (of which Seurel unreservedly approves) and Frantz's 'fantasmagories' (which he deprecates).

Unlike Seurel, who was 'un enfant malheureux, et rêveur et fermé' (p.104), and Valentine, who seems to have had a harsh and cheerless time of it, Meaulnes, Yvonne and Frantz de Galais seem to have had particularly indulgent parents. M. de Galais lets Frantz live alone, from a very early age, in his own little house and gratifies his every whim. Meaulnes's mother, we learn, 'était riche et lui passait toutes ses volontés' (p.92), one of which has been the somewhat unusual request to purchase the municipal schoolhouse where his dead schoolteacher father had taught for twenty years (p.116). The fact that Seurel becomes a schoolteacher like his own two parents, and that, in her first conversation with him, Yvonne de Galais declares: 'J'enseignerais, moi aussi, si M. de Galais voulait! J'enseignerais les petits garçons, comme votre mère...' (p.108) — all this can be seen as evidence of the fascination childhood continues to exert over their thoughts and feelings. As we have seen, even Jasmin Delouche, who cannot put childlike things behind him quickly enough, continues happily to haunt the village school.

Frantz has had so idyllic a childhood that like Peter Pan he wants forever 'to be a boy and have fun'. Seurel thinks that to roam the countryside in his own little house on wheels is, for Frantz, the ideal solution: 'Il avait accepté cette existence sauvage, pleine de risques, de jeux et d'aventures. Il lui avait semblé recommencer son enfance...' (p.83). Yvonne also wishes that time would stand still and that childhood need never end; speaking to Seurel amidst the desolation of Frantz's forlorn little house, she declares: 'Moi je passe ici bien souvent. Les petits paysans des environs viennent jouer dans la cour comme autrefois. Et je me plais à imaginer que ce sont les anciens amis de Frantz; que lui-même est encore un enfant et qu'il va revenir bientôt avec la fiancée qu'il s'était choisie' (p.143). How Meaulnes view his childhood, we never really know. We can only infer that parts of it, at least, were happy when he responds, with evident enchantment, to the chance evocation of old memories. After entering *le château mystérieux* for the first time:

> Il lui sembla bientôt que le vent lui portait le son d'une musique perdue. C'était comme un souvenir plein de charme et de regret. Il se rappela le temps où sa mère, jeune encore, se mettait au piano l'après-midi dans le salon, et lui, sans rien dire, derrière la porte qui donnait sur le jardin, il l'écoutait jusqu'à la nuit... (p.38)

He recalls that same memory just after his marriage, when he sees Yvonne standing beside the piano:

> "Ma mère, lorsqu'elle était jeune femme, penchait ainsi légèrement son buste sur sa taille pour me parler... Et quand elle se mettait au piano..."
> Alors Mlle de Galais proposa de jouer avant que la nuit ne vînt... (p.137)

In the course of this short conversation, almost the only one

Meaulnes and Yvonne ever have together as man and wife, Yvonne spends much of the time displaying memories of her childhood as a form of homage to her husband. The 'choses merveilleuses dont elle était chargée' (p.136) include: 'ses jouets de petite fille, toutes ses photographies d'enfant: elle en cantinière, elle et Frantz sur les genoux de leur mère, qui était si jolie... puis tout ce qui restait de ses sages petites robes de jadis...' (ibid.).

These young adults looking back are the mirror-images of their childhood selves looking forward. In all the talk about 'aventures' and 'folies' or 'fantasmagories', the dreams and visions of the three male protagonists are domesticated to a degree. On Meaulnes's wedding-day, Seurel imagines that throughout the village, 'dans chaque maison, le feu de la salle à manger fait luire tout un reposoir de joujoux vernis. Fatigué de jouer, l'enfant s'est assis auprès de sa mère et il lui fait raconter la journée de son mariage...' (p.130). Yvonne tells Seurel that when Frantz was still a small child, 'il avait voulu une maison pour lui tout seul, loin de tout le monde dans laquelle il put aller jouer, s'amuser et vivre quand cela lui plairait... Et quand cela lui plaisait, un jeudi, un dimanche, n'importe quand, Frantz partait habiter dans sa maison comme un homme. Les enfants des fermes d'alentour venaient jouer avec lui, l'aider à faire son ménage, travailler dans le jardin. C'était un jeu merveilleux!' (p.143). Meaulnes's secret dream, cherished from early childhood, is of waking to find himself in his own home; listening to the girl playing the piano at *la fête étrange* 'il put imaginer longuement qu'il était dans sa propre maison, marié, un beau soir, et que cet être charmant et inconnu qui jouait du piano, près de lui, c'était sa femme...' (p.46). In a paragraph excised from the account of their week-end spent in the country, Meaulnes muses about Valentine whom he likens to 'une ménagère dans sa demeure':

> Meaulnes la regardait faire avec un plaisir étrange. Il se plaisait à penser que leur bonheur était un bonheur d'enfant et leur ménage un ménage de gamins de Ste Agathe. Il se sentait en ménage comme lorsque les enfants

tracent par terre, dans la petite cour, sous les bouquets du mur, trois petits compartiments: la chambre, la salle à manger et la cuisine et s'imaginent, durant une indéfinie soirée, la chambre à coucher, que vraiment tout est arrivé, et que le soir ils couchent là, dans le petit carré où il y a d'écrit: le lit. (p.191)

One wonders why this charming little passage was suppressed. It can only have been because of the emotional charge carried by that final word of the paragraph. Just such a charge is carried in the final paragraph of Alain-Fournier's first published work, 'Le Corps de la femme', a prose-poem which defines his feminine ideal as a gentle natural figure, gracefully moving and chastely clad at all times, disrobing only when she has retired behind the alcove-curtains to take her place in the bed where babies are made and babies are born. The bed, in times of peace, is also where most people die, and to this dark theme I shall return in the following chapter.

5. Structure and Signification

One of the most damaging charges recurrently levelled at *Le Grand Meaulnes* is that it is incoherent. Since it first appeared, critics and scholars have argued that it constitutes an uneasy alliance between realism and fantasy. Each of these distinctive elements has found supporters. Gustave Lanson, for example, writing in the newspaper *Le Matin* as early as 24 December 1913, declared he was unmoved by the fantastic — or what he described as the *conte bleu* — features of the novel but was much impressed by those passages 'où l'auteur, se réveillant de ses songes, consent à regarder avec une ironie clairvoyante les gens de son village ou, avec une âme émue de la beauté des choses, les aspects de la campagne'. On the other hand, Gide much preferred the first hundred pages, which he found full of 'une irressaisissable fraîcheur' and felt that 'le reste du livre court après cette première émotion virginale, cherche en vain à s'en ressaisir... Je sais bien que c'est le sujet même du livre; mais c'en est aussi le défaut, de sorte qu'il n'était peut-être pas possible de le "réussir" davantage'.[3] Denis Saurat's view was that only the first fifty pages of the novel are an unqualified success, and that, thereafter, it 'rather flounders to an unfortunate ending', adding that the subject is 'really only matter for a short story'.[4]

Still other critics have opted neither for the 'realism' nor the 'fantasy' but have deprecated Alain-Fournier's alleged failure to blend the two. In a notoriously hostile article in *La Nouvelle Revue Française* of 1 November 1938, Marcel Arland declared: '*Le Grand Meaulnes* a curieusement vieilli... De plus en plus ses deux éléments fondamentaux: son réalisme et son symbolisme épris de mythes, divergent et se nuisent... Fournier, balancé sans

---

[3] *Journal, 1889-1939* (Gallimard, Bibliothèque de la Pléiade, 1948), p.1150. Entry for 2 January 1933.

[4] *Modern French Literature, 1870-1940* (Dent, 1946), p.105.

doute dans sa propre vie entre ces deux éléments, n'a pas su les unir dans son œuvre' (p.820). And in a book of essays, published that same year, Albert Thibaudet, contrasting 'authentic' adventure with 'novelettish' adventure, concluded that '*Le Grand Meaulnes* a peut-être cent pages de trop, celles où le romanesque prolonge l'aventure quand l'aventure a donné tout son effet: le romanesque est jeté sur les marcs de l'aventure pour en faire une seconde cuvée'.[5]

Clearly, if any of the above criticisms can be substantiated, then *Le Grand Meaulnes* is irredeemably flawed. If there is, indeed, a sharp demarcation between the realistic and the so-called 'fantastic' elements of the novel, then Alain-Fournier has failed to implement the programme he outlined to Rivière in August 1906 when he declared: 'Mon livre futur sera peut-être un perpétuel va-et-vient insensible du rêve à la réalité' (*6*, p.323). And if the novel is so lacking in unity that any or all of its parts are superior to the whole, or detachable from the whole without undue detriment to either, then whatever else it may turn out to be, *Le Grand Meaulnes* cannot be taken seriously as a work of art.

To make as stark a demarcation as most of the above critics seem to have done, between the world of *la fête étrange* and the world of everyday Sainte-Agathe, seems to me to be a serious misreading of the text: it suggests that insufficient attention has been paid to that idiosyncratic vision of the omnipresent narrator which we analysed in chapter 2 of this study. The land-scape we see is not a neutral photograph, it is very much 'un coin de la création vu à travers un tempérament' and that tempera-ment is wistful, romantic and poetic. Seurel inhabits a haunted countryside in which the wind and the weather are forever suggesting that the world his senses apprehend is not necessarily the only one. For him, as for Alain-Fournier, dreams are not confined to the world of sleep, they are 'l'immense et imprécise vie enfantine planant au-dessus de l'autre et sans cesse mise en rumeur par les échos de l'autre' (*6*, p.323). The enchantment with which Meaulnes views events at *la fête étrange* and that with which Seurel records the scenes in the village blacksmith's

[5] *Réflexions sur le roman* (Gallimard, 1938), pp.77-78.

shop, or the cry of a shepherdess resounding faintly across the silence to set his imagination vibrating differ in degree, not in kind. For Seurel, until he is confronted with the death of Yvonne in all its brutal physicality, life is a blend of 'rêve' and 'réalité'; he consistently perceives what Alain-Fournier described in an unpublished letter to André Lhote as 'la merveille étroitement insérée dans la réalité'. Of course, not all of the characters in the novel perceive the world in the poetic way that Meaulnes and Seurel do, and the fact that the latter take so long to find the lost domain while all manner of prosaic personages know all along where it is, is a calculated irony the significance of which I shall examine later.

If the 'vision and voice' of Seurel are two crucial unifying elements in the narrative, another, no less potent, is the effect of the theme or themes on its structure. Even the more distinguished of the earlier critics of *Le Grand Meaulnes* appear to have experienced considerable difficulty in discerning either: Thibaudet seems to have considered it an example of the episodic adventure novel *à la française*, while Gide acknowledges there is a theme but says nothing about structure. Latter-day critics have more than made up for this deficiency. In the first structuralist essay on the subject, 'A Structural Diptych in *Le Grand Meaulnes*', Hedi Bouraoui comes briskly to the point: '*Le Grand Meaulnes* furnishes the modern critic with an admirable example of the identification of the structure of the work with its intention',[6] the argument being definitively worked out in the book which followed five years later (*21*). For Dr Bouraoui, *Le Grand Meaulnes* combines poetic intensity with a boldness of form which anticipates *Les Faux-Monnayeurs* and *le nouveau roman*: its 'true' subject is 'la création poétique' and the principal male characters are all, in their different ways, creative artists; the least convincing of these is Seurel, irredeemably flawed by his bookish sentimentality; the most authentic are the virtuoso mime-artiste Ganache, encapsulating his tragic view of the human condition with his inspired enactment of 'l'homme qui tombe', and Meaulnes himself, whose diary-entries and letters from Paris constitute the 'proof' that he is

[6] *French Review*, XLII (December 1968), 233.

potentially a gifted writer who could, in time, compose prose-poems on the urban scene to vie with Baudelaire's *Spleen de Paris*. Each of the three parts of the novel has its own 'foyer' (or microcosm), these being respectively 'La Chambre de Wellington', Ganache's pantomime and Meaulnes's Journal. The central image is the Quatre-Routes, the cross-roads which appear, both figuratively and literally, at major crises in each hero's life. In case the reader is unpersuaded by this, Dr Bouraoui identifies, for good measure, 'la profusion d'allusions et d'emprunts littéraires': Meaulnes is compared to Molière's Dom Juan and to Hamlet while the discomforts he experiences en route for the lost domain are likened to Christ's sufferings on the road to Golgotha. In the key chapter of the novel, 'La Chambre de Wellington', affinities are detected with Baudelaire's 'Correspondances', Valéry's sonnet 'Les Pas', and links postulated with Yorick, Shakespeare's First Gravedigger, Ophelia and Laurel and Hardy. All that is missing to make the *fête étrangissime* complete, as far as I can judge, is a reference to Alice's 'curiouser and curiouser'.

Another structuralist critic, Marie Maclean, is both more perceptive and rather more persuasive. Her subtly argued and finely detailed study, *Le Jeu suprême* (*31*), is full of insights too numerous to consider here. There are occasions when the structuralist's compulsion to find a geometrical analogue for the literary work seems designed to divert attention more towards the critic's ingenuity than to the work being analysed. The 'deep' structure that Bouraoui perceives in *Le Grand Meaulnes* is a decapitated cone. Marie Maclean proposes a whole series of con-centric circles, representing the sequence in which the reader is made aware of the character-pairings in the narrative: so Seurel and Meaulnes, whose relationship is the first we read about, form the outer ring enclosing all the others, and the Meaulnes-Valentine relationship, the last we allegedly perceive (what about Meaulnes and his daughter?) forms a tiny circle in the very centre. One's objection to this proposed structure is that it does not really correspond to one's experience of reading the novel, when the revelations are consecutive: neither does it do adequate justice to the complexity of the inter-relationships experienced *concurrently* by individual characters. A pattern of ever-decreasing circles looks pleasing enough as a symmetrical design, but it does not, in my view, begin to convey the anguish of either Meaulnes or Seurel who love two people simultaneously, or render the elusive poetry of which the whole work is compounded. Rather more convincing is her proposal for restructuring the original table of contents. She demonstrates, first, how carefully patterned is that original order: three sections, divided into seventeen, twelve and seventeen chapters respectively, each section further divided by a major character's running away — Meaulnes from school, Frantz from the village, Meaulnes from Yvonne — and she demonstrates that each of these *fugues* brings about a dramatic change in time and *dramatis personae*. However, she suggests that the true structure of the work is two equal parts of exactly twenty-two chapters each, with a pivotal section at the epicentre. This centre is the circus-performance on the village-square where, to conclude the proceedings, the young stranger appears without his bandage and stands revealed as Frantz de Galais. This particular structure exemplifies the central, unifying theme of the whole novel which is, in her view, the tension between *paraître* and *être*, between Illusion and Reality. This undoubtedly is a motif of considerable importance (though I wonder, *en passant*, whether the 'real' Frantz de Galais is not, like Mallarmé's *pitre châtié*, the character wearing his make-up) but, as I shall now try to demonstrate, it is part of a rather more complex whole — a whole for which I shall not try to find the appropriate geometrical equivalent.

Let us consider first the most clearly sign-posted of the contrasts which bind the work together: *la fête étrange* of Part One and *la partie de plaisir* of Part Three. The aura of enchantment which plays around *le château mystérieux* is not left unbroken. Frantz makes his petulant entrance, in an atmosphere of gloom and storm, and peremptorily decrees 'c'est fini; la fête est finie' (p.54). The children's reign over events is usurped by tipsy adults and the magic spell, which has been tenuous throughout (see pp.87-88 below) is finally broken:

...les moins bons des invités, qui peut-être avaient bu, s'étaient mis à chanter. A mesure qu'il s'éloignait, Meaulnes entendait monter leurs airs de cabaret, dans ce parc qui depuis deux jours avait tenu tant de grâce et de merveilles. Et c'était le commencement du désarroi et de la dévastation. Il passa près du vivier où le matin même il s'était miré. Comme tout paraissait changé déjà... — avec cette chanson, reprise en chœur, qui arrivait par bribes:

> *D'où donc que tu reviens, petite libertine?*
> *Ton bonnet est déchiré*
> *Tu es bien mal coiffée...*

et cette autre encore:

> *Mes souliers sont rouges...*
> *Adieu, mes amours...*
> *Mes souliers sont rouges...*
> *Adieu, sans retour!* (pp.55-56)

The snatches of song are both suggestive and prophetic; the clear hint of licentiousness in the first points to the scenes to come, in which Valentine will insist that she is just such a 'petite libertine' and Meaulnes will feel he has fallen forever from grace; the reiterated message of finality in the refrain of the second is, though he does not know it at the time, directly applicable to him. The *fête* is, indeed, at an end, and any attempt to reconstitute it is doomed to fail.

Just such an attempt is made to celebrate the reunion of Meaulnes with Yvonne, eighteen months later, when Seurel's Uncle Florentin organizes his *partie de plaisir* on the banks of the Cher, where 'on s'était efforcé comme jadis de mêler riches et pauvres, châtelains et paysans' (p.121). While waiting for Yvonne to arrive, Meaulnes looks in vain, with mounting despair and, at the same time, with perverse satisfaction, for vestiges of the original *fête*. As the late summer sun goes down the sky, Meaulnes's increasingly urgent questions discover that the old manor house has been demolished, the lake has been filled in, the yacht on which he sailed with Yvonne has been sold, the bric-à-brac of *la chambre de Wellington* has been thrown away. Of *la fête étrange*, only one vestige seems to remain, the least hoped for yet the most appropriate. As the party-goers stand temporarily silent, they hear, in the distance, a farm-worker singing the ballad 'Mes souliers sont rouges':

> Meaulnes avait levé la tête et écoutait. Ce n'était rien qu'un de ces airs que chantaient les paysans attardés, au Domaine sans nom, le dernier soir de la fête, quand déjà tout s'était écroulé... Rien qu'un souvenir — le plus misérable — de ces beaux jours qui ne reviendraient plus. (p.127)

Yvonne de Galais too has survived, of course, as lovely, as gentle and as pure as she was at the time of the first meeting, indeed, Seurel convinces himself that she arrives in precisely the same fashion as she did on that first occasion. But Meaulnes is no longer the same. Now he is only too well aware that he has forfeited his right to return to the lost domain. When he first wakes up at *la fête étrange*, it is to find his bedroom 'éclairée par les lanternes vertes' (p.40), the traditional colour of freshness and innocence. Between *la fête étrange* and *la partie de plaisir* he has seen lanterns of another colour and with quite different significance in the back streets of Bourges: 'Il y avait çà et là l'enseigne d'une maison louche, une lanterne rouge' (p.166). It is to that world, frequented by Army officers boasting of their extra-marital 'adventures' as they swill their liquor, that he believes he has consigned Valentine — in whose (now lost) honour *la fête étrange* was originally staged. The contrast between Innocence and Experience could scarcely have been more starkly marked.

Each of the three parts of *Le Grand Meaulnes* sounds a different key-note: in Part I, it is enchantment and high hope; in Part II, it is bafflement and mounting frustration; in Part III, it is disillusionment and desolation. In none of the three parts does the keynote entirely dominate: near the very beginning of Part I, for example, Seurel expresses that elegiac mood which is his particular stock-in-trade when he laments lost childhood felicity (see above, pp.52-53) and, as we have just observed, reality displaces illusion at *la fête étrange* rather earlier than the circus-performance which is central to Marie Maclean's structure. Hopes continue to rise in both Parts II and III but they are dashed with insistent regularity and increasing brutality. Meaulnes is by no means the only victim. The world grows appreciably darker for Seurel too and immeasurably smaller. One of the chief attractions of the childhood holidays he used to spend at his Uncle Florentin's in Le Vieux-Nançay, was being made aware of long journeys undertaken across vast and misty distances. He is compelled to realize that he is losing this childhood quality of vision at the end of his abortive expedition through the woods to find the lost domain by himself:

> Je suis arrivé sans y penser à l'extrémité des Communaux, que j'avais toujours imaginée infiniment loin. Et voici à ma droite, entre des piles de bois, toute bourdonnante dans l'ombre, la maison de garde. Deux paires de bas sèchent sur l'appui de la fenêtre. Les années passées, lorsque nous arrivions à l'entrée du bois, nous disions toujours, en montrant un point de lumière tout au bout de l'immense allée noire: "C'est là-bas la maison de garde; la maison de Baladier." Mais jamais nous n'avions poussé jusque-là. Nous entendions dire quelquefois, comme s'il se fût agi d'une expédition extraordinaire: "Il a été jusqu'à la maison du garde!"
>
> Cette fois, je suis allé jusqu'à la maison de Baladier, et je n'ai rien trouvé. (pp.88-89)

He has learned the melancholy lesson which is expounded in the opening four lines of Baudelaire's great valedictory poem 'Le Voyage':

> Pour l'enfant, amoureux de cartes et d'estampes,
> L'univers est égal à son vaste appétit.
> Ah! que le monde est grand à la clarté des lampes!
> Aux yeux du souvenir que le monde est petit!

This raises crucial questions: are the child's eyes in fact

deceived? Or do they actually look, as poets like Vaughan, Traherne and Wordsworth insist, at a different (and possibly truer) reality? Was *la fête étrange* 'real' or was it 'illusory', merely a trick of the light? If it truly happened — and the old-fashioned silken waistcoat provides Meaulnes with the evidence that it did, just as the suggestive power of the narrative persuades *us* that it did — why is it so difficult, indeed impossible, for Meaulnes to find his way back? There are a number of practical reasons which are, in themselves, not altogether implausible: the fact that Meaulnes travelled to and from the domain literally in the dark, the fact that he and Seurel have only a tenuous grasp of geographic detail, the fact that their self-imposed code of secrecy inhibits Meaulnes and Seurel from asking the remarkable number of relatives and acquaintances who know all along where the château is. The additional fact that the rest of the guests at *la fête étrange* are not, like Meaulnes, haunted by thoughts of it ever after prompts one to ask why it made such a dramatic and enduring impact on *him*.

One obvious reason is that it is only Meaulnes who falls in love with Yvonne de Galais and only Meaulnes who extracts from her the promise that she will wait in the château till he returns. There is, however, another reason, much less obvious and, seemingly, never properly understood either by Meaulnes or Seurel. Arriving at the domain for the first time, Meaulnes passes between two white posts and enters a drive which leads between the fir trees: 'Il y fit quelques pas et s'arrêta, plein de surprise, troublé d'une émotion inexplicable... un contentement extraordinaire le soulevait, une tranquillité parfaite et presque enivrante, la certitude que son but était atteint et qu'il n'y avait plus maintenant que du bonheur à espérer...' (p.35). Where have we read something like this before? I suggest that is in Proust's *Du côté de chez Swann*, when the middle-aged Marcel describes the emotions that are unaccountably triggered off one winter's day when he begins to eat a piece of madeleine cake dipped in tea:

A l'instant même où la gorgée mêlée des miettes de gâteau toucha mon palais, je tressaillis, attentif à ce qui se passait

d'extraordinaire en moi. Un plaisir délicieux m'avait
envahi, isolé, sans la notion de sa cause. Il m'avait aussitôt
rendu les vicissitudes de la vie indifférentes, ses désastres
inoffensifs, sa brièveté illusoire, de la même façon
qu'opère l'amour, en me remplissant d'une essence
précieuse: ou plutôt cette essence n'était pas en moi, elle
était moi. J'avais cessé de me sentir médiocre, contingent,
mortel. D'où avait pu me venir cette puissante joie?[7]

Marcel has a sharp-edged, probing mind, and by a sustained
effort of the will, is able to identify the cause of his euphoria.
The madeleine taste he savours in middle age matches the taste
of the same sort of cake served to him years before, in distant
childhood, by his aunt. The two widely separated moments are
like a pair of electric terminals: once connected, a powerful
current flows between them.

Neither Meaulnes nor Seurel has Marcel's sharpness of mind
nor tenacity of purpose. For them, Meaulnes's ecstasy remains
'inexplicable' — except that the explanation is promptly
supplied: it is no different from Marcel's. As Meaulnes proceeds
on his way up the drive, he reflects:

C'est ainsi que, jadis, la veille des grandes fêtes d'été, il se
sentait défaillir, lorsqu'à la tombée de la nuit on plantait
des sapins dans les rues du bourg et que la fenêtre de sa
chambre était obstruée par les branches.

"Tant de joie, se dit-il, parce que j'arrive à ce vieux
pigeonnier, plein de hiboux et de courant d'air!..."

Et fâché contre lui-même, il s'arrêta, se demandant s'il
ne valait pas mieux rebrousser chemin et continuer
jusqu'au prochain village. Il réfléchissait depuis un
instant, la tête basse, lorsqu'il s'aperçut soudain que l'allée
était balayée à grands ronds réguliers comme on faisait
chez lui pour les fêtes. Il se trouvait dans un chemin pareil
à la grand-rue de La Ferté, le matin de l'Assomption!...

(pp.35-36)

[7] *A la recherche du temps perdu* (Gallimard, Bibliothèque de la Pléiade, 1954),
Vol.1, p.45.

This is Meaulnes's first 'epiphany' — to use the term Joyce employs for the sudden upsurge of euphoria experienced by *his* young hero. Soon after, there is another, the sound of distant piano music borne on the wind, which transports him out of present time into the past, when he would sit till dusk outside the door of the room where his mother was playing her piano. Significantly, when he hears that piano music again, and identifies the player as a blonde young lady, he chooses to sit listening to her in an *adjoining* room.

Much of Meaulnes's enchantment at *la fête étrange* is with the swirl of events, with the sense that his secret childhood dream has at last come true, but a potent ingredient in the heady brew which so ravishes his senses is the feeling that he is outside Time: the high delight generated even before the *fête* is under way and recharged by the piano-music, emanates from his private past; the costume he is wearing when he espies his reflection in the pool comes from an age before his birth, as do the coaches in the courtyard and the *objets d'art* strewn around *la chambre de Wellington*. The combination of all these factors is quite fortuitous, just as the re-emergence of some of Meaulnes's most cherished memories is quite involuntary. The emotions he experiences at the *fête* are genuine enough, and his perceptions are real and true. They are also, by their very nature, transient, and even had he been able to reassemble all the actors, stage-properties and lighting-effects of the original celebration, there is no guarantee that his 'first, fine, careless rapture' could have been relived.

While Meaulnes may be entranced, if occasionally ill at ease when the *fête étrange* is actually going on, Seurel, recording the events long afterwards, is more circumspect. He does not reveal that he knows the final outcome when he is in the process of describing the *fête*, but there are clear signals from within the narrative that Meaulnes has *not* been transported into another world. The first set of such 'signals' comprises the regular reminders of decay and dereliction in the setting: the iron bars which should have protected the windows of *la chambre de Wellington* have long since rusted away (p.37); Meaulnes is convinced the château has been unoccupied for ages (p.40) and observes that 'tout paraissait vieux et ruiné' (p.41). However, even though, as is later confirmed, the chateau is not long for this world, it remains very much *of* this world. This is established by the further 'signals' transmitted by Seurel's syntax. As has already been noted, when he has recourse to figurative language, he is particularly fond of the conjunction *comme*. This has the effect not only of making the analogy more explicit but of drawing attention to the fact that an analogy is being drawn. One may be momentarily delighted or dazzled by the aptness or strangeness of the analogy but the original subject is not lost from view. *Comme*, as used by Seurel, consistently implies 'as if': he knows, and we know, he is engaged in make-believe. This sense of make-believe is regularly reinforced by the use of the verb *sembler*: Yvonne's first glance at Meaulnes 'semblait dire...' (p.49), 'on allait aborder, semblait-il' (ibid.), or by the use of the conditional tense: 'on eût pu se croire au cœur de l'été' (ibid.), 'la jeune fille s'y promènerait' (ibid.), 'jusqu'au soir on entendrait' (ibid.), 'on se fût cru transporté sur la pelouse verte et taillée de quelque champ de courses en miniature' (p.52). After each of these brief flights of fancy, the narrative regularly returns to the delapidated château or the Sologne countryside: our senses are never disorientated as they are when we read Rimbaud's *Illuminations* or a Surrealist poem.

It follows, from this 'reading' of *la fête étrange*, that I take Meaulnes to be mistaken in his conviction that he was somehow privileged to participate in it because of his pristine purity: 'j'en suis persuadé maintenant, lorsque j'avais découvert le Domaine sans nom, j'étais à une hauteur, à un degré de perfection et de pureté que je n'atteindrai jamais plus' (p.119). He wanders into the château purely by chance, and it is purely by chance that he is enraptured where and when he is by the phenomena of involuntary memory. One of the several cruel ironies of the novel is that there is, in fact, no demonstrable connection between virtue and reward. Meaulnes may punish himself for his transgressions, but his loyal friend Seurel, and his pure and virtuous wife Yvonne, are punished very much more severely: the one loses everything he loves most, the other loses her life. If there are any 'winners' at the end of it all, they are those bitterly antagonistic polar-opposites Frantz de Galais and Jasmin Delouche, neither of whom is a paragon of virtue.

This pair engages intermittently in a campaign of mutual recrimination in which other characters also take sides. Frantz does not equivocate: 'C'est ce Delouche surtout qui me déplaît. Quelle idée de faire l'homme à dix-sept ans! Rien ne me dégoûte davantage...' (p.74). Delouche is equally forthcoming; Frantz is to blame for everything: 'C'est celui-là qui a tout fait. C'est lui qui a rendu Meaulnes insociable, Meaulnes qui était un si brave camarade!' (p.95). At the time, Seurel almost agrees: 'Me voici presque de leur avis. Tout aurait sans doute autrement tourné si nous n'avions pas considéré l'affaire d'une façon si mystérieuse et si tragique. C'est l'influence de ce Frantz qui a tout perdu...' (ibid.). Later, Seurel is more categoric: 'Delouche et Boujardon n'avaient pas tort. Que de mal nous a fait ce Frantz romanesque!' (p.115). Meaulnes takes the totally opposite view; for him Frantz is 'le garçon le plus merveilleux du monde!' (p.164). The two heroines, on the other hand, seem resolutely anti-Romantic. Working-class Valentine dismisses Frantz's description of the fairy-tale reception and of the little house in the woods awaiting her as whimsical fantasy. The aristocratic Yvonne de Galais dreams of becoming a village schoolmistress and of teaching her pupils common-sense: 'J'apprendrais aux garçons à être sages, d'une sagesse que je sais. Je ne leur donnerais pas le désir de courir le monde... Je leur enseignerais à trouver le bonheur qui est tout près d'eux et qui n'en a pas l'air...' (p.109). The rights and wrongs of the argument are not easy to determine: Frantz is flamboyant in his words and actions, but he has promised no more than the truth to Valentine, and it was that Romantic imagination which Delouche and Seurel so deplore which brought *la fête étrange* into being; Yvonne's teaching plans sound commendable enough, but had they really been implemented in Meaulnes's case, he would never have run away from school and found his way to her side in the first instance. The parent-figures are equally innocent or equally guilty: had M. de Galais not been so indulgent he would not have paid for the *fête* to be staged, and had Madame Meaulnes not been so ready to grant her son's

every whim, he would not have been allowed to travel, either to
Sainte-Agathe or onward to Paris; on the other hand, had M.
Seurel not been so insistent on having *his* way, Meaulnes would
have been selected to accompany him to fetch the grandparents
from the railway station, and would not have been goaded into
his act of rebellion against authority.

For his part, Meaulnes is in no doubt who is the most culpable
of all the characters: it is Valentine. When she denounces Frantz
de Galais for being out of touch with reality, Meaulnes rounds
on her vehemently: 'Ah! poursuivit-il avec fureur, quel mal vous
nous avez fait, vous qui n'avez voulu croire à rien. Vous êtes
cause de tout. C'est vous qui avez tout perdu! tout perdu!'
(p.164). Characteristically — and ironically — he is unwilling or
unable to accept that he himself is in no small measure to blame
for keeping so boorishly silent at Sainte-Agathe, when to have
been more open would have paid rich dividends, and for taking
so literally both Frantz's melodramatic oath and Valentine's
equally melodramatic threat to become a prostitute (when
nothing Meaulnes has said or done prevents her from returning
to her craft as a seamstress). Even more ironic is the fact that it is
Seurel, the most selfless and best-intentioned of all the
characters, who bears most reponsibility for causing undue
distress to the very friends he most seeks to serve: on occasions,
he is silent when he should have spoken (p.135), or speaks when
he should have kept silent (p.119), he fails to react to the
mention of the names Moinel and Le Vieux-Nançay when
Meaulnes first relates his adventure (pp.32 and 44), he turns
away too precipitately from Baladier's gamekeeper's lodge
instead of questioning him (p.89), and, in the summer following
la fête étrange, he even contrives to spend the holidays with
Uncle Florentin and his nine cousins (p.98) and never once
mentions his quest for *le château mystérieux*. But there is a
further irony even blacker than this: even if he had found
Yvonne sooner, had revealed the whereabouts of Valentine to
either Frantz or Meaulnes in good time, and even if, as a
consequence, Meaulnes had stayed at Les Sablonnières and
quietly cultivated his garden, Yvonne would have died in just the
same circumstances.

When one re-reads the novel, one finds any number of advance warnings of how frail and vulnerable she is. When he first meets her, 'Meaulnes eut le temps d'apercevoir, sous une lourde chevelure blonde, un visage aux traits un peu courts, mais dessinés avec une finesse presque douloureuse' (p.49) and he notes that 'ses chevilles étaient si fines qu'elles pliaient par instants et qu'on craignait de les voir se briser' (p.50). As the party begins to break up in disorder, 'Meaulnes songea un instant à la jeune fille inquiète, pleine de fièvre et de chagrin, qui entendrait chanter dans le Domaine, jusqu'au milieu de la nuit, ces paysans avinés' (p.57). The feverishness, which has not previously been mentioned, is associated with her more and more insistently as the narrative proceeds (pp.146, 147, 150 and 151). Seurel's very first impression is that she is 'la plus grave des jeunes filles, la plus frêle des femmes' (p.108) and he notes 'Je ne remarquai qu'un défaut à tant de beauté: aux moments de tristesse, de découragement ou seulement de réflexion profonde, ce visage si pur se marbrait légèrement de rouge, comme il arrive chez certains malades gravement atteints sans qu'on le sache' (ibid.). Just before she meets Meaulnes at the *partie de plaisir*, Seurel notes that 'malgré ses joues et ses pommettes roses, il y avait autour de ses yeux, à son front, par endroits, une pâleur violente où se lisait tout son trouble' (p.123); after the wedding, her face is 'plein de faiblesse et d'angoisse' (p.137); when on the evening of the wedding, Frantz's owl-call summons Meaulnes out into the woods, Yvonne runs out in pursuit, trips and falls, and arrives at his side with 'le front écorché au-dessus de l'œil droit et du sang figé dans les cheveux' (p.139); she is 'échevelée, pleurante, salie', (ibid.) and, not surprisingly, when Seurel calls three days later to pay his respects it is to discover that 'Yvonne de Galais était alitée, avec une fièvre violente' (p.140). Several weeks pass before she is well enough to see him and he finds her 'tout enfiévrée... avec de vives taches rouges sous les yeux, et dans un état d'agitation extrême' (p.141). Two months later, when they visit together *la maison de Frantz*, she is still 'toute pâlie, toute tourmentée' (p.142). When they meet in the garden outside Les Sablonnières in late August, Seurel remembers that 'Elle me tendit une main brûlante' (p.146). Critics who dismiss

Yvonne as the conventional Ice Maiden of some Gothic fairy-tale have clearly not paid close enough attention to the text: the iciness so carelessly attributed to her comes only with her death.

For her funeral, she is dressed in 'son admirable robe de velours bleu sombre, semée par endroits de petites étoiles d'argent, mais il a fallu aplatir et friper les belles manches à gigot maintenant démodées' (p.153), but she is no more allowed a Romantic ending than is Emma Bovary: 'le médecin craint la décomposition rapide, qui suit parfois les embolies. C'est pourquoi le visage, comme tout le corps d'ailleurs, est entourée d'ouate imbibée d'alcool' (ibid.). For the first and only time, Seurel can take Yvonne in his arms, but it is only to carry her down the narrow stairs to the coffin below:

> Agrippé au corps inerte et pesant, je baisse la tête de celle que j'emporte, je respire fortement et ses cheveux blonds aspirés m'entrent dans la bouche — des cheveux morts qui ont un goût de terre. Ce goût de terre et de mort, ce poids sur le cœur, c'est tout ce qui reste pour moi de la grande aventure, et de vous, Yvonne de Galais, jeune femme tant cherchée — tant aimée... (p.153)

The bitter contrast with *la fête étrange* first pointed out in *la partie de plaisir* is now finally driven home, and that this was deliberately calculated is spelled out in a recently discovered note Alain-Fournier sent to Péguy on 7 July 1913: '...le peu de volupté qu'il y a, le peu de lanterne magique, de fantasmagorie, de ballet russe et d'aventure anglaise, est racheté par un si long regret, une si étroite peine' (5, p.134).

The repeated reminders of Yvonne's fragility, and the details of her wretched death, are by no means the only references in the novel to death and physical disability. Meaulnes's father is dead and his younger brother also, 'mort un soir au retour de l'école, pour s'être baigné avec son frère dans un étang malsain' (p.6); Delouche's father is dead, the deaths of Yvonne's father and mother are curtly reported in the course of the narrative; Aunt Moinel's husband dies after *la fête étrange*, all her children are dead, and her home has been transformed into a miniature mausoleum 'où les murs étaient tapissés de vieux diplômes, de portraits de défunts, de médaillons en boucles de cheveux morts' (p.112); Meaulnes's abrupt departure from Sainte-Agathe school is immediately preceded by a funeral procession over the village cross-roads which, the narrator points out, seems calculated to mock their hopes of happiness: 'Le cercueil, amené dans une charrette à bœufs, était déchargé et posé sur une dalle, au pied de la grande croix où le boucher avait aperçu naguère les sentinelles du bohémien!' (p.92). References to sickness and mutilation abound: Seurel's childhood is blighted by coxalgia; Jenny, daughter of the local *châtelaine* is 'admirable, mais folle et toujours enfermée' (pp.26-27; in an early draft, her brain is permanently damaged when her father throws her out of a window); Meaulnes damages his knee when he runs away from school and limps into *le domaine étrange*; Ganache's body is 'le plus lamentable qu'on puisse imaginer' (p.39); when he performs in front of the villagers at Sainte-Agathe, he walks 'recroquevillé sur son ventre comme par une colique' (p.81); his acts consist of imitating a spastic unable to stand upright and of slowly disembowelling a stuffed doll (p.82); Madame Delouche's hand has been badly burned and is permanently twisted out of shape; Yvonne's baby daughter has to be delivered with the use of forceps with the result that 'la petite fille avait la tête blessée et criait beaucoup' (p.149). These details are evenly scattered throughout the narrative and not confined, as the structuralist critics suggest, to the period following the circus performance.

The lost domain is not immune: the clue which points Seurel towards it is an inscription on a family tombstone; the missing title of *le domaine sans nom*, 'Les Sablonnières', is doubtless indicative that the heroes' high hopes are built on sand. Right in the heart of *la fête étrange*, within the magical *chambre de Wellington*, Ganache's pitiful face provides powerful intimations of mortality: 'ses yeux glauques et louches, sa moustache retombant sur sa bouche édentée faisaient songer à la face d'un noyé qui ruisselle sur une dalle' (p.39); as the celebrations break up in confusion, Frantz tries to blow his brains out. A 'dream world' this may be, but it bears within it the stigmata of nightmare. Like Meaulnes himself, Death is another uninvited guest at *le domaine perdu* and has inscribed there the message that stands out in Poussin's famous painting *Et in Arcadia ego*: 'even in Arcadia, there I am'. Alain-Fournier has fully implemented the intention he outlined in an unpublished letter sent to André Lhote on 19 December 1909: 'Je voudrais que dans le livre que j'écris il y eût de plus en plus pénétrant ce goût de la mort entré dans mon royaume.'

To attach undue importance to the morbid elements of *Le Grand Meaulnes* would be to misrepresent it as seriously as to ignore them altogether, or to over-stress such other aspects as the dream-like features of *la fête étrange* or the vignettes of village life. Its various themes cannot be encapsulated within a simple label or, as I have tried to argue, adequately represented in a single structuralist diagram. The fullest and fairest formula I have yet encountered to do justice to the hidden complexities of this deceptively simple-looking work is that provided at the end of Timmermans' excellent study of Alain-Fournier's style: 'le plus admirable poème de l'enfance et de la nature, de l'aventure et de l'adolescence, de l'amour et de la mort' (*36*, p.89).

6. Interpretation and Evaluation

Though Alain-Fournier insisted: 'Je n'ai pas pensé à faire un livre de moral. J'ai voulu faire un livre vivant',[8] critics have never ceased to probe *Le Grand Meaulnes* to uncover its system of moral values and decode its secret 'message'. The 'message' which has been most regularly discovered within it and, certainly, the 'message' which has been most eloquently canvassed by its proponents is a religious, indeed, a specifically Christian, one: Meaulnes is seen as 'un poète... un homme religieux, torturé par la destinée humaine, meurtri par la vie, secoué par l'inquiétude métaphysique' and the novel is 'une œuvre toute résonnante de l'appel de Dieu' (*14*, p.204).

If this is, indeed, the 'message' of *Le Grand Meaulnes*, one is bound to say that it is well hidden. Explicit references to the church, to its representatives and its doctrines are remarkably few in number and invariably parenthetical: Seurel as a small child attends Mass (p.4), 'une bonne sœur' visits Frantz de Galais when he is ill in his caravan (p.85), Meaulnes and Yvonne are married in the old family chapel (p.131), and, looking back from some way off, Seurel sees a priest about to call at Les Sablonnières, where Yvonne is dying or perhaps already dead (p.151). Meaulnes's one specific comment on the church, as he walks around — and, very pointedly, *outside* Bourges Cathedral — is positively hostile; he feels for it 'une crainte de paysan, une répulsion pour cette église de la ville, où tous les vices sont sculptés dans des cachettes, qui est bâtie entre les mauvais lieux et qui n'a pas de remède pour les plus pures douleurs d'amour...' (p.166).

The Christian apologist's counter to such objections is not to probe beneath the text of *Le Grand Meaulnes* in order to lay bare its deeper structures; it is to go outside the text of the novel altogether. Consider, for example, the following characteristic

[8] Unpublished and undated letter to his cousin, André Feur. See *1*, pp.cxvi-vii.

comments:

> Qui niera la possibilité d'une interprétation mystique du *Grand Meaulnes* n'aura qu'à ouvrir la *Correspondance* et plonger dans le mystère d'une vie toute secouée par l'appel de Dieu (*14*, p.227)

and

> L'interprétation chrétienne du *Grand Meaulnes* peut vraiment se justifier. Elle s'appuie sur plus d'un passage de la Correspondance. Si Alain-Fournier a mis dans son œuvre 'toute son âme déchaînée' il faut croire qu'il y a mis aussi ses tourments religieux. (*13*, p.207)

These are particularly striking instances of the 'intentionalist' fallacy, the erroneous belief that an author's practice must inevitably correspond with his theory; the gulf between the two is often very wide indeed. In any event, the quotations normally cited to 'prove' that *Le Grand Meaulnes* is a Catholic novel are lifted from letters he wrote in 1909 and 1910 when he was planning to express his recent religious crisis in *Le Jour des noces*. As I have tried to demonstrate, by the time he came to plot the final version of *Le Grand Meaulnes*, these plans were radically modified.

Although it is clearly an exaggeration to describe *Le Grand Meaulnes* as 'une œuvre toute résonnante de l'appel de Dieu', and certainly a distortion of the internal evidence of the text as it stands to claim that it is an apologia for any specific *Christian* creed, the novel, nevertheless, does express preoccupations which are symptomatic of many a religious spirit. Pre-eminent amongst these is the conviction that one's powers of vision are intimately linked with one's state of moral or sexual purity. Meaulnes persuades himself that he has somehow forfeited the right to re-enter *le domaine perdu* because he has betrayed his personal faith: 'un homme qui a fait une fois un bond dans le paradis, comment pourrait-il s'accommoder ensuite de la vie de tout le monde? Ce qui est le bonheur des autres m'a paru dérision. Et lorsque, sincèrement, délibérément, j'ai décidé un jour de faire comme les autres, ce jour-là j'ai amassé du remords pour longtemps...' (p.118). The self-disgust so evident in this utterance has, in fact, more than one cause: he is remorseful by this stage not only because he feels he has betrayed Yvonne but also because he has betrayed Valentine whom he also loved, after his fashion, and who, on occasions, brought him 'tant de paisible bonheur' (p.161). However, orchestrating the theme of irretrievably lost innocence, he goes on, '... j'en suis persuadé maintenant, lorsque j'avais découvert le Domaine sans nom, j'étais à une hauteur, à un degré de perfection et de pureté que je n'atteindrai jamais plus. Dans la mort seulement... je retrouverai peut-être la beauté de ce temps-là' (p.119), which echoes the despairing conclusion of the last of his Paris letters to Seurel: 'Peut-être quand nous mourrons, peut-être la mort seule nous donnera la clef et la suite et la fin de cette aventure manquée' (p.99) — yet further expressions of the powerful death motif I outlined in the preceding chapter.

These utterances do not provide the soundest of bases on which to construct a religious model of Meaulnes, the more so if one compares what he says with what he actually does. He evidently has no confidence that his sense of contamination can ever be cleansed by confession, and it is not so deeply ingrained as to prevent him from proposing marriage to the newly discovered Yvonne de Galais just a week later. If to practice what one preaches is any criterion of a genuine religious spirit, then Seurel is a rather more convincing contender. He is as pure in thought as Meaulnes and rather purer in deed. He has the same highly developed sense of personal honour and after revealing Meaulnes's secret adventure to the other village-boys (in the chapter eloquently entitled 'Je trahis'), he is deeply distressed: 'Le soir, tout seul dans ma chambre, je me couche bien vite pour étouffer le remords que je sens monter du fond de ma tristesse' (p.96). As we have noted already (see above pp.30-31), he regards the whole matter of human happiness and marital consummation with a mixture of awe, reverence and fear. Of all the major characters, he is by far the most ascetic.

The cult of purity which particularly preoccupies the Christian

apologist for *Le Grand Meaulnes* is of consuming interest also to
the psycho-analytical critic. The majority of these have treated
the novel as though it were a print-out from the inner reaches of
the author's sub-conscious. In a review article in 1946, Marie
Forestier made the fairly obvious point that the novel expressed
Alain-Fournier's marked reluctance to face the realities of adulthood.[9] For Robert Champigny, the three main male characters
are three aspects of a single personality: Seurel is the 'ethical'
hero, Frantz is the 'pseudo-Romantic' hero and Meaulnes is the
'Symbolist' hero (*24*). The most profound, and, at the same
time, most ingenious, psycho-analysis of the novel to date has
been that carried out by Michel Guiomar. Adopting the techniques and terminology pioneered by Gaston Bachelard, he
effectively demonstrates that the submerged theme of *Le Grand
Meaulnes* is the main characters' search to rediscover and re-
establish their lost childhood home: Frantz succeeds, Meaulnes
half-succeeds, but Seurel fails completely, and this explains why
the dominant mood of the novel is nostalgia and regret:
'Comparable à la perte d'un parent, l'arrachement à la maison
natale a d'ailleurs conféré à tout le roman la hantise d'un climat
maternel anciennement dévasté' (*29*, p.224). Daniel Grojnowski
also argues that *Le Grand Meaulnes* 'doit être lu comme la
description d'un univers mythique, la projection d'un paysage
intérieur' (*27*, p.721), while Claude Vincenot proceeds from the
same starting-point — '*Le Grand Meaulnes* est un roman
d'aventure trouble et compliqué' (*39*, p.296) — but pursues a
rather different course: he suggests that Alain-Fournier's
fascination with images of the sea might in part be explained by
the phonetic identity between the terms *mer* and *mère*, identifies
the objects Meaulnes discovers on the bed at *la fête étrange* as
male and female symbols, and sees Freudian significance in the
fact that after drawing back the curtains of the alcove and
getting into bed, he should suddenly think of his mother. A
more thorough-going Freudian analysis has been undertaken by
Derek Savage in his still-to-be-published study *The Mystery of
Meaulnes*, in which he observes that mentally disturbed patients

obsessed with secret drawings, as Meaulnes is with his secret map, are regularly found to be sketching more or less crude representations of the place 'where babies come from'; the white posts between which Meaulnes passes on his approach to the domain are seen as legs, the array of open doors and windows are standard symbols for feminine orifices, and the fact that he is limping painfully as he makes his entrance recalls archetypal Œdipus with his damaged foot. Some of these studies are more convincing than others but all tend to be reductive and to see *Le Grand Meaulnes* as evidence in the case-history of the allegedly traumatized author.

But not all critics of *Le Grand Meaulnes* see its heroes' cult of purity as evidence of deep neurosis. Writing in the paper *Combat*, for example, René Vincent took a radically different approach:

> La signification profonde du *Grand Meaulnes* est... sans doute finalement la pureté. S'il est une catégorie de la littérature où l'on puisse le ranger, c'est probablement dans la littérature de chevalerie, dont il ressuscite, à une époque chargée de matérialisme, le splendide idéalisme. *Le Grand Meaulnes*, c'est dans la féerie des aventures, le mystère resurgi en plein XXe siècle, des chevaliers, c'est leur même idéal. C'est un des plus beaux romans d'amour qui aient été écrits non parce que l'amour de Meaulnes et d'Yvonne de Galais est un amour inaccompli, un amour romantique triste, mais parce qu'il est un exemple parfait de l'amour courtois... c'est aux aventures de notre littérature chevaleresque qu'il nous fait irrésistiblement songer: aux exploits mystiques des chevaliers de la Table Ronde en quête du Graal.[10]

Alain-Fournier was certainly familiar with one of the Arthurian romances, *Le Roman de Tristan et Yseult*, in the modern adaptation by Joseph Bédier. He bought it as a New Year's present to himself in January 1913 and wrote to tell Rivière that the opening chapters had moved him to the depths

[10] '*Le Grand Meaulnes*, roman de chevalerie', *Combat*, 32 (February 1939).

of his being (7, p.418). One of these chapters is 'La Quête de la Belle aux Cheveux d'Or': in it, King Marc summons all the knights of his court and tells them he will marry the far-distant Princess from whose impossibly fair head one golden hair has been brought to him across the perilous seas. The greatest knight of the court, Tristan, swears a solemn vow to set out on the quest to bring the fair Yseult back to Tintagel or die in the attempt. Purity, however, can scarcely be said to be the dominant theme of this particular romance, because Tristan and Yseult fall in love with a passion so demanding that it must needs be requited in defiance of all the laws of man or God.

A closer parallel between *Le Grand Meaulnes* and a different tale of chivalry is suggested by Frederick Locke in his admirable essay 'The desire and pursuit of the whole' (*30*). He proposes *Le Conte del Graal* by Chrétien de Troyes: the hero, Percival, the first of the questers for the Holy Grail, leaves his home in response to the call of high adventure, and discovers a castle more beautiful than anything of which he has ever dreamed; there he has an encounter no other knight has experienced but, because he fails to ask a crucial question at the appropriate moment, he awakens next morning to find himself back in the drab world of everyday; his one desire thereafter is to find the enchanted castle again and complete the adventure he has begun. This archetypal tale, which is re-enacted in such haunting poems as the *Ballad of True Thomas* and *La Belle Dame sans merci*, is, argues Locke, essentially about a quest for the meaning of existence, and so is Alain-Fournier's novel:

> *Le Grand Meaulnes* is the story of a *recherche de l'Absolu*... This desire and pursuit of the whole lies behind the pattern of the Quest which I have outlined, and in it is reflected the quest of adolescence and its end. For it is a Quest for the Absolute, for the ultimate meaning of man's life, for a way out of the fragmentation of the Wasteland: a search for wholeness. But unfortunately all the images of the Absolute have a way of slipping and sliding. As Boethius remarked, an image of the real Good is something that cannot bring us to Beatitude. And he was echoed

by Dante when the Italian poet spoke of 'those false images which never fully keep their promises'. (*30*, p.146)

Le Grand Meaulnes as a repository of archetypal characters and situations is the subject of a richly suggestive essay by Harry Goldgar. Taking his cue from Jacques Rivière, who was the first to suggest that Alain-Fournier's 'sources d'inspiration sont d'ordre populaire' (*4*, p.33), he considers 'the folklore motifs that are imbedded in the peasant consciousness' (*26*, p.87). He points out that many of the motifs of *Le Grand Meaulnes* are listed in Stith Thompson's *Motif-Index of Folk Literature* (6 vols, Bloomington, 1955-58): the 'magic power of children', 'wisdom learned from children', 'enchanted princess in castle', 'quest for faraway princess', 'question on quest: where is lost princess?', 'vow not to marry until quest concluded', magic castles or fairy castles of various sorts, 'directions on quest given by peasant and wife', 'choice of roads', 'quest for things seen in a dream', 'quest for unknown, vanished beloved', 'quest for girl hero has seen in a dream', 'horses determine road to be taken', 'horse allowed to go as it pleases, finds unknown person'. All these motifs are linked with one initiation archetype, charting the hero's progress from childhood, through adolescence and into maturity. To buttress his attractive argument, and to explain Meaulnes's 'call to adventure' in Part I of the novel, he quotes most tellingly from Joseph Campbell's classic study of the heroic monomyth, *The Hero with a Thousand Faces* (New York, 1961, p.58):

This first stage of the mythological journey — which we have designated the 'call to adventure' — signifies that destiny has summoned the hero and transferred his spiritual center of gravity from within the pale of his society to a zone unknown. This fateful region of both treasure and danger may be variously represented: as a distant land, a forest, a kingdom underground, beneath the waves, or above the sky, a secret island, lofty mountain top, or profound dream state; but it is always a place of strangely fluid and polymorphous beings, unimaginable torments, superhuman deeds, and impossible delight. The hero can go forth of his own volition to accomplish the adventure...; or he may be carried or sent abroad by some benign or malignant agent... The adventure may begin as a mere blunder...; or still again, one may be only casually strolling, when some passing phenomenon catches the wandering eye and lures one away... Examples might be multiplied, ad infinitum, from every corner of the world.

The archetypal hero's journey to the Underworld or the Unconscious, or the 'Realm of the Mothers' or *le pays sans nom*, is seen as a literary representation of those initiation ceremonies which, in primitive societies, are enacted in some isolated hut or cabin out in the bush. In each case, the psycho-drama is essentially the same: the individual has to die as a child before being reborn as a fully-fledged adult. Goldgar argues that on the archetypal level, Frantz's owl-call signifies a crisis in Meaulnes's nearly accomplished initiation and this is not finally completed, Goldgar argues, until he takes his child in his arms and so fully integrates his consciousness. On the other hand, 'Poor Frantz, though he has his Jeanne [*sic*] in his toy house at the end, seems to be doomed, to what nightmare of dis-integration we can only guess' (*26*, p.97).

Goldgar follows this with another challenging quotation, this time from the anthropologist Mircea Eliade, who reminds us that initiation into adulthood in antiquity and in primitive societies was a *religious* ritual: 'The experience of initiatory death and resurrection not only basically changes the neophyte's fundamental mode of being, but at the same time reveals to him the sacredness of human life and of the world, by revealing to him the great mystery, common to all religions, that men, with the cosmos, are the creation of the Gods or of Superhuman beings'.[11] In the contemporary world, Goldgar suggests, writers write — and the rest of us read — books which, though apparently secular 'in fact contain mythological figures camouflaged as contemporary characters and offer initiatory

[11] *Rites and Symbols of Initiation*, trans. W.R. Trask (New York, Harper, 1965), p.19.

scenarios in the guise of everyday happenings' (Eliade, p.135). He concludes:

> Alain-Fournier was conscious of the superficially secular character of his novel: 'Mon livre sera peu chrétien. Puisque, sans doute, ce sera un essai, sans la Foi, de construction du monde en merveille et en mystère' [7, p.108]. But he must somehow have known that the supernatural character of his hero and the archetypal character of the hero's initiation sprang from, and would appeal to, a fundamental religious instinct. Perhaps the universal popularity of *Le Grand Meaulnes* is due most of all to its profoundly religious, collective and archetypal character.
>
> (*26*, p.99)

An interesting variant of Goldgar's approach is that followed by Elaine Cancalon who argues that *Le Grand Meaulnes* has much in common with a large number of fairy-tales and with *The Sleeping Beauty*. Observing, for example, how regularly the number 'three' recurs in the classic fairy-tale — three wishes, three brothers, three tasks to be accomplished, three blind mice, three bears — she demonstrates the remarkable frequency with which it features in Alain-Fournier's novel: it occurs five separate times in Chapter I alone (pp.3, 4, 5, 7, 8); when Meaulnes returns to school after his inexplicable absence, he announces to M. Seurel: 'Voici trois nuits que je ne dors pas' (p.21); as Meaulnes loses his way in the Sologne countryside 'il lui fallut bien traverser trois prés' (p.31); when he first arrives at *le domaine mystérieux*, 'il pouvait être trois heures de l'après-midi' (p.35); as he hides behind the fir-trees of the drive to avoid being detected, he sees 'trois fillettes avec des robes droites qui s'arrêtaient aux genoux' (p.37); he enters the main building accompanied by two small boys and 'ils sont tous les trois arrivés à la porte d'une grande salle' (p.43); he overhears at dinner that Frantz and his fiancée 'ne seront pas là, demain, avant trois heures' (p.44); at the *fête étrange*, 'trois bateaux de plaisance accostaient, prêts à recevoir les promeneurs' (p.49); the solemn pact proposed by Frantz is pledged by three boys; Meaulnes sends three letters to Seurel from Paris; at *la partie de plaisir*, Yvonne makes three wishes: 'Que Frantz revienne s'il n'est pas mort. Qu'il retrouve ses amis et sa fiancée; que la noce interrompue se fasse et peut-être tout redeviendra-t-il comme c'était autrefois' (p.126). To make three wishes in the world of fairy-tale is to expose oneself to mortal danger and Yvonne, of course, dies not long after. Other fairy-tale conventions in the novel include Meaulnes's repeated attempts to set out for the lost domain at midnight, and the insistence that the hero should draw up his plan of return alone and find his way back to the secret place unaided: to invoke the aid of the non-initiated is to break the spell. Acknowledging her indebtedness to E.K. Schwartz's 'Psychoanalytic Study of the Fairy Tale' (in *The American Journal of Psychotherapy*, 1956), Elaine Cancalon follows the line that fairy-tales are most often figurative expression of the problems of growing up and attaining a mature and integrated personality; the monsters the hero regularly encounters on his travels are images from his own infantile past; the dark forest which so frequently needs to be traversed is an analogue for the depth and obscurity of the psyche; the safe emergence on the other side and the eventual marriage of hero and heroine who 'live happily ever after' is the symbolic recognition that the personality has been made whole and maturity achieved. Divergences from fairy-tale norms in Alain-Fournier's novel are indications, she argues, of psychological malaise: Meaulnes is reluctant to achieve self-unity, hence his hesitations and wrong turnings; the fact that he and Yvonne do not live happily ever after, and the lack of harmony between the triad of heroes who together constitute a single complex psyche, provide eloquent evidence that the author himself has yet to attain a definitively integrated personality.

Whatever the merits of these various critical approaches, they seem to me to have two major shortcomings. Firstly, they concentrate almost exclusively on Meaulnes who is, for long periods, absent altogether from the narrative and, in so doing, they virtually ignore Seurel who, as narrator and actively participating character, is present throughout. Secondly, in searching for deep structures, or coded messages, or affinities with other modes of writing, they tend to lose sight of the text of *Le Grand Meaulnes* itself. When all is said, however close the parallels between Alain-Fournier's work and *romans courtois* or folktales or fairy-stories, it is not, in fact, any of these things. It is a novel, with a poetically rendered rural setting, and it addresses itself *directly* to what the literary analogues we have been considering all treat in their various figurative ways: the painful transition from adolescence into maturity. *Le Grand Meaulnes* is the work Alain-Fournier had (still unformed) in mind when he wrote to Rivière in April 1908: 'J'aimerais qu'il y eût, dans mes livres, un livre ou un chapitre intitulé "La Fin de la Jeunesse" (7, p.194).

Some of the most distinctive features of adolescence are virtually ignored in *Le Grand Meaulnes* or handled rather perfunctorily. Because the parental figures, for the most part, treat their children most indulgently, there is never any serious conflict between the youthful protagonists and Authority: Meaulnes's resolve to ignore M. Seurel's decision that Mouchebœuf will accompany Seurel to the railway station is the only serious instance of teenage rebellion in the novel; the schoolboys' collective decision later to play truant and go bird-nesting is treated by M. Seurel as a sort of game into the spirit of which he cheerfully enters by donning hunting-clothes and arming himself with an old pistol (p.87). With the somewhat prudish Seurel as narrator, a discreet veil is drawn over the problems most adolescents have to solve in coming to terms with their sexual development. Delouche poses the only serious threat to Seurel's determinedly asexual outlook and, as we have seen, he counters this by censoring the details of his subversive conversations. The physical consequences of Meaulnes's marriage to Yvonne produce from Seurel a flurry of rhetoric on which the most appropriate comment is doubtless this quotation from the preface to Keats's *Endymion*: 'The imagination of a boy is healthy, and the mature imagination of a man is healthy; but there is a space of life between, in which the soul is in a ferment, the character undecided, the way of life uncertain, the ambition thicksighted'. For the rest, however, some of the principal preoccupations of sensitive adolescents of any era are exquisitely rendered.

Both in their thoughts and actions, Meaulnes and Seurel, for good or ill, are governed by that same obsessive sense of honour which characterizes the youthful heroes of courtly romance or Corneille's Rodrigue or Hugo's Hernani and has for its most lyrical spokesman Shakespeare's Hotspur:

> By heaven methinks it were an easy leap
> To pluck bright honour from the pale-faced moon...
>
> (*Henry IV*, 1.iii.201)

To their credit — and to their detriment — they share youth's unwillingness to compromise and its inability to take a detached, ironic view. Unlike Rimbaud — who may well in any case, have been affecting more *insouciance* than he actually felt when he declared 'On n'est pas sérieux quand on a dix-sept ans' — they take every promise or threat quite literally and they believe their sorrows are both unique and eternal. As George Eliot observes in *Middlemarch* 'no age is so apt as youth to think its emotions, partings and resolves are the last of their kind'. They regularly express youth's irrational but overwhelming conviction that ineffable happiness must surely be just around the corner or over the brow of the next hill, that today may have turned out just the same as yesterday but — 'Demain matin, peut-être!...' (p.35) and 'Ah! frère, compagnon, voyageur, comme nous étions persuadés, tous deux, que le bonheur était proche, et qu'il allait suffire de se mettre en route pour l'atteindre!...' (p.79). As happens again and again both in Rimbaud's poems and his prose, the high hopes with which Alain-Fournier's characters set out are blighted when they ultimately arrive: this is as true of small-scale incidents — such as the delicious taste Seurel savours in advance while waiting to drink from the bottle of lemonade chilled in the river when, finally, 'il ne revenait guère à chacun... qu'un peu de mousse qui piquait le gosier et ne faisait qu'irriter la soif' (p.102) — as it is of the high drama of Meaulnes's reunion with Yvonne at *la partie de plaisir*: 'Je m'étais fait de ce jour tant de joie à l'avance! Tout paraissait si parfaitement concerté pour que nous soyons heureux. Et nous l'avons été si peu' (p.121). At moments, as when Meaulnes drives his horse and cart across the landscape silvered over with hoar-frost, or when Seurel sweeps downhill on his bicycle in golden high summer, the narrative communicates the sheer joy of being young in 'le vierge, le vivace et le bel aujourd'hui'. But more dominant still is the note of heart-break, resounding more and more insistently as the narrative proceeds but, as Jacques Rivière points out in a recently discovered preface to *Le Grand Meaulnes*, discernible even at *la fête étrange*:

> Le Domaine... c'est celui de l'adolescence. Il est habité par tous les fantômes, mais personnifiés, agissants, vivants, que l'adolescence imagine et projette. L'amour y palpite encore innocent bien que meurtrier. Et la tristesse de l'adolescence, la plus profonde, la plus inapaisable, puisqu'elle ne sait pas de cause, y monte doucement comme une fumée sur la lande. Je ne sais rien dans la littérature qui soit plein à la fois d'autant de rêves et d'autant de fuites et d'évanouissements que *Le Grand Meaulnes*. Je ne retrouve rien dans ma mémoire qui soit en même temps aussi enchanté et aussi désenchanté.[12]

Each of the three main characters, for their different reasons, seems to share the sentiments expressed by Alain-Fournier in a letter he wrote to Rivière in June 1909: 'Je suis las et hanté par la crainte de voir finir ma jeunesse' (*7*, p.300). Aware that they stand mid-way between childhood and maturity, they seem more aware of the penalties of growing up than of its rewards. Frantz reacts most petulantly of all and behaves childishly from first to last. Meaulnes makes the most determined bid to become an adult, though both he and Yvonne clearly hope that their married life will re-enact the dreams they dreamed as children. Seurel, the 'good' child schooled never to rebel and the loyal friend who never thinks to betray, is the all-round loser: he yearns for the peace and the wonderment of lost childhood (*40*) and he mourns the passing of youth. When Meaulnes leaves Sainte-Agathe for Paris, he is left alone 'avec l'impression que,

[12] *Bulletin des amis de Jacques Rivière et d'Alain-Fournier*, 3 (1976), 34.

dans cette vieille voiture, mon adolescence venait de s'en aller pour toujours' (p.93). When Meaulnes deserts Yvonne in order to find Valentine, alone in the deserted schoolroom 'je pensais de même que notre jeunesse était finie et le bonheur manqué' (p.145). When Yvonne dies, he grieves for her but also for a whole lost world: 'Tout est pénible, tout est amer puisqu'elle est morte. Le monde est vide, les vacances sont finies. Finies, les longues courses perdues en voiture; finie, la fête mystérieuse...' (p.152). About what has happened to Seurel in later life, we can only speculate, but it seems all too evident that nothing that has happened to him subsequently can compensate him for the loss of childhood and youth, and that his only hope of consolation is to write about it. This provides both the *raison d'être* of the narrative enterprise and its dominant elegiac tone.

That *Le Grand Meaulnes* has now achieved the status of a minor classic can scarcely be denied: apart from the phenomenal sales-figures it continues to enjoy year by year either in its original French form or in the thirty-three different languages into which it has been translated, it has been the subject of higher degree theses in a dozen of the world's universities, is regularly prescribed as an examination text in Western Europe and America and, as we have seen, it has been considered from every manner of critical angle. It has been lyrically praised and contemptuously dismissed (see *1*, pp.172-77 for a representative selection of views). The eulogistic end of the critical spectrum is occupied by such fervent supporters as Havelock Ellis who has little patience with *Le Grand Meaulnes*'s detractors: 'there are people to whom it seems a simple and insignificant story, just as there are people who inhale in vain the most exquisite fragrance of flowers, or... find trivial the music of Mozart'.[13] And there are some, like the critic Edmond Pilon, to whom it has a 'magic' which simply defies analysis: 'Il y a des œuvres d'une fragilité de pastel, et si diaphanes, si douces, si spécialement subtiles et tendres, qu'on ne peut pas les toucher du doigt sans les froisser. L'aventure de Meaulnes appartient à cette sorte d'œuvres.'[14]

[13] Preface to *The Wanderer* (New York, Houghton Miflin, 1928), p.xxvii.

[14] *Alain-Fournier*, in the series 'Les Amis d'Alain-Fournier' (Paris, Champion, 1920), p.28.

I simply do not believe that the undeniable 'magic' of *Le Grand Meaulnes* is impervious to analysis, any more than I believe that its cause is best served by asserting that it is beyond criticism. Its major shortcomings seem to me to have to do with the working-out of the plot. I find it entirely plausible that Meaulnes and Seurel should experience such inordinate difficulty in locating the lost domain, but I remain somewhat incredulous that when Meaulnes goes back, it should have been so utterly transformed. In twenty months, the main buildings have been demolished, and a lake large enough for three yachts to sail across has been filled in to extend the game-reserves of local huntsmen (p.106): a large labour force must have worked many hours of overtime! And in spite of Martin Sorrell's ingenious argument that the structuring of the narrative in Part III expresses Seurel's urge to assert his new-found power over Meaulnes (*35*), I still find it difficult to justify the positioning of Meaulnes's secret journal in the novel and the way the original version has been so savagely censored. Alain-Fournier's letters and the excised versions of the Meaulnes-Annette (Valentine) liaison graphically record a relationship rich in human interest and provide all the justification wavering critics could reasonably require for Meaulnes's bizarre conduct after his wedding. The material Alain-Fournier actually produced provides unimpeachable evidence that he had the literary ability to handle it; that he chose, in the end, to suppress it can be explained as failure of artistic nerve.

At the opposite end of the critical spectrum from Ellis and Pilon is Henry de Montherlant who, in June 1936, laconically dismissed Alain-Fournier's novel in the preface he wrote for *Anna, premier visage*, a novel submitted by a young writer, Lucy Arny, to a literary prize-panel of which he was a member: 'Lorsque j'eus ingurgité quatre ou cinq resucées du *Grand Meaulnes* (la resucée d'un livre insignifiant, on voit ce que ça peut être), trois ou quatre resucées de Rimbaud et deux ou trois resucées de Valéry, sans parler du reste, je repris mes esprits en tournant les feuilles de *Anna, premier visage*. Ceci, enfin, n'était pas de la littérature...' (Clearly, with Montherlant as her friend and literary protector, Mlle Arny had no need of enemies.) In

November 1938, in a review article in *La Nouvelle Revue Française*, the critic Marcel Arland was to condemn *Le Grand Meaulnes* for being 'un bric-à-brac de thèmes en vogue et déjà rongés de littérature' (p.820); but the most heavily charged bill of indictment remains that drawn up by the American academic, Donald Schier. Having dismissed the plot as 'a creaking collection of old tricks', the coincidences responsible for the Valentine episode for being 'of a kind which no serious novelist since Dickens has dared to use', Alain-Fournier's representation of adolescence as 'entirely artificial' and his characters as 'merely incredible', he concludes that where other critics discern in the novel youth's capacity for idealization and an exaltation of Christian purity, he regretfully finds 'only one half penny-worth of tawdry adventure to an intolerable deal of saccharine' (*33*, pp.130-32).

Setting aside, for the moment, the sarcastic and unnecessarily strident tone of the accusers, one is bound to concede that there would appear to be some substance in some of their charges. Certainly — perhaps inevitably, in the case of a young writer who was also a voracious reader — one can hear clear echoes from works he is known to have admired. From *Pelléas et Mélisande*, the first words Golaud speaks to the golden-haired heroine — 'N'ayez pas peur... Je ne vous ferai pas... Oh! vous êtes belle!' — and almost the last words he speaks when he sees his brother Pelléas kissing that golden hair as it cascades down from Mélisande's casement — 'Vous êtes des enfants... Vous êtes des enfants' — are heard again in 'La Rencontre' as they were, significantly, in Alain-Fournier's meeting with Yvonne de Quiévrecourt in real life. From Nerval's *Sylvie*, the episode of young people dressing up in the costumes of yesteryear, and from Fromentin's *Dominique*, a young lover's thoughts of suicide over unrequited love and the name Augustin. From Rimbaud's prose-poem 'Aube', the line 'Rien ne bougeait encore au front du palais' which seems to be picked up in Seurel's 'Rien ne bouge encore dans ce clair paysage d'hiver'.[15] From *La Porte étroite*, the notion of the hidden journal which

[15] See J. de Lutri, 'Rimbaud and Fournier: the end of the quest', *Romance Notes*, X (Winter 1977), 154.

finally provides the explanation of the central character's bizarre behaviour, though even when Gide used this device, it was already 'rongé de littérature'. Certainly, Alain-Fournier's plot makes significant use of coincidences, though the meeting between Meaulnes and Valentine outside the de Galais house in Paris is much more plausible than Frantz's arrival, at a particularly opportune moment, on two separate occasions, at Sainte-Agathe. And certainly, there are moments of melodrama in each of the three parts of *Le Grand Meaulnes*, invariably involving Frantz. He was the last of the characters to be created and, like many another last-minute *trouvaille*, he has, arguably, created as many technical problems as the invention of him promised to solve. He is an absolutely vital cog in the machinery of the plot — nothing would turn without him — but his consistently extravagant words and actions have attracted more outspoken criticism than any other feature of the novel.

In concentrating, as they invariably have done, on deficiencies in plot or characterization, one cannot help wondering if Alain-Fournier's principal detractors are being a little obtuse. If a critic's chief criterion for evaluating human behaviour is, as it seems to be for Donald Schier, the behaviour of clean-limbed American sophomores, then few novels or plays are going to be spared his censure. The activities at the court of King Lear are, one would like to believe, 'very different from the home-life of our own dear Queen' and we suspend our critical disbelief in matching them largely because we are beguiled by Shakespeare's verse. By the same token, if we pay rather more attention to the delights of what I have called Seurel's 'poetry' and less to the actions of the characters, we might do the narrative more justice. It has been well observed that 'the logic of the novel is emotional not rational' (*24*, p.48) and also that 'the novel is one in which images are more important than events' (*37*, p.482). This prompts the crucial question which, ever since the novel first appeared, has continued to exercise scholars and critics: what *kind* of work is *Le Grand Meaulnes*? Until we have resolved that, we can never be sure that we are judging it by the appropriate criteria. Wayne Booth seems to me to provide the answer in the course of a general discussion in his invaluable

Rhetoric of Fiction (University of Chicago Press, 1961) when he suggests that what might well seem 'a botched novel' could prove to be a 'successful romance' (p.37). Perhaps the true place of *Le Grand Meaulnes* is not, after all, alongside those French *romans personnels*, like *René* or *Sylvie* or *Dominique* to which it has most frequently been compared, but with such English romances as *Great Expectations* or *Wuthering Heights* which Alain-Fournier so enthusiastically admired (9, p.185).

Ultimately, however, the critic's attitude to *Le Grand Meaulnes* is not likely to be determined by technical considerations at all. The rapturous acclaim of its admirers, and the rancorous contempt of its detractors, suggest a degree of personal *animus* which I find rare in pronouncements on literary texts. I suspect that this may well depend on whether the passing of our own childhood and youth is, to us, a matter of regret, relief, indifference or ambivalence — as it is to Seurel.

Bibliographical Note

EDITIONS

Since October 1913, when *Le Grand Meaulnes* was first issued in book form, there have been many editions of the plain text published often with ornate illustrations; these are too numerous to list here. There are three competent school editions each with an elementary critical apparatus: two separate French editions in Livre de Poche, the first published in 1964, edited by Yves Rey-Herme, replaced in 1983 by the edition of Daniel Leuwers; an English edition of similar calibre was published by Methuen in 1968, edited by Michel Sanouillet and Pierre Robert. There are two more advanced editions with a fuller critical commentary and a selection of *inédits*:

1. *Le Grand Meaulnes*, with introduction and notes by Robert Gibson (London, Harrap, 1968, pp.cxxxvi + 197).
2. *Le Grand Meaulnes*, with introduction, notes and choice of variants by Claude Hertzfeld (Paris, Nizet, 1983, pp.406).

A full critical edition of the novel is still awaited. All the drafts and variants are stored in the archives of the Association des Amis de Jacques Rivière et Alain-Fournier. This was founded in 1975 and issues four bulletins each year frequently containing previously unpublished material by or about each author. Numbers 30, 31 and 33, for example, provide a very detailed bibliographical account of the books and articles devoted to *Le Grand Meaulnes* since 1913.

3. 'Le Pari': Chapter IV of his unfinished second novel, *Colombe Blanchet*, *La Nouvelle Revue Française*, 1 December 1922.
4. *Miracles*: poems, short stories and a suppressed chapter of *Le Grand Meaulnes* (Paris, Gallimard, 1924).

LETTERS

Indispensable for deeper understanding of the writer, his work and his background.

5. *Alain-Fournier — Charles Péguy: Correspondance, 1910-1914* (Paris, Fayard, 1973).
6. *Correspondance avec Jacques Rivière*, Vol.1, January 1905-December 1906 (Paris, Gallimard, 1948).
7. *Correspondance avec Jacques Rivière*, Vol.2, January 1907-July 1914, idem.
8. *Lettres d'Alain-Fournier à sa famille, 1898-1914* (Paris, Emile-Paul, 1949; since 1971, Fayard).

9. *Lettres au petit B.* (Paris, Emile-Paul, 1930; since 1971, Fayard). B. was
    A.-F.'s friend René Bichet.

The above collections are by no means definitive. Thirteen further letters in the
Rivière-Fournier collection have yet to be published and a number of excisions
made by Isabelle Rivière in the earlier texts now need to be restored.

BIOGRAPHY

Because of the close connection between Alain-Fournier's life and work, nearly
every biography of the author provides some account of the genesis of *Le Grand
Meaulnes*. Unless a distinctive line is indicated, it can be assumed that the
biographer's approach is general and non-partisan.

10. Becker, A., *Itinéraire spirituel d'Alain-Fournier* (Paris, Corrêa, 1946).
     One of the best argued of the Christian interpretations.
11. Gibson, R., *The Land without a Name* (London, Paul Elek, 1975). The
     fullest study in English, superseding *The Quest of Alain-Fournier*
     (London, Hamish Hamilton, 1953).
12. Gillet, H., *Alain-Fournier* (Paris, Emile-Paul, 1948). By one of the most
     devoted of the older Fournieristes: now somewhat outmoded but full of
     charm.
13. Jöhr, W., *Alain-Fournier, le paysage d'une âme* (Neuchâtel, A la
     Baconnière, 1972). Christian apologetic but includes some perceptive
     stylistic comments.
14. Léonard, A., *Alain-Fournier et 'Le Grand Meaulnes'* (Paris, Desclée de
     Brouwer, 1943). Christian apologetic.
15. Loize, J., *Alain-Fournier, sa vie et 'Le Grand Meaulnes'* (Paris,
     Hachette, 1968). Monumental, particularly rich in detail on A.-F.'s
     family antecedents and his Army service, but ineffective as a reference
     work because it lacks an index.
16. Rivière, I., *Images d'Alain-Fournier* (Paris, Emile-Paul, 1938). A.-F.'s
     sister's recollections of their childhood; sensitive and poetic.
17. ——, *Vie et passion d'Alain-Fournier* (Monaco, Jaspard, Polus et Cie,
     1964). Concentrates on A.-F.'s later love-life, in particular his affairs
     with Jeanne Bruneau and Simone Casimir-Périer, his last mistress.
     Contains many previously unpublished letters and extracts from his
     diaries.
18. Rivière, J., Introduction to *4* above. Remains one of the most
     penetrating articles ever written on A.-F. and his work.

CRITICAL STUDIES

19. Bales, R., 'Geography and language in Nerval and Alain-Fournier' in
     Studies in French Literature presented to Henri Godin (Coleraine, New
     University of Ulster, 1984), 136-43. Admirable comparative study of the
     limits of language.
20. Bastaire, J., *Alain-Fournier ou l'anti-Rimbaud* (Paris, Corti, 1978).
     Well-argued and illustrated comparative study.

21. Bouraoui, H.A., *Structure intentionnelle du 'Grand Meaulnes': vers le poème romancé* (Paris, Nizet, 1974). Structuralist study arguing unconvincingly that the 'true' artists of the novel are Meaulnes and Ganache.

22. Cancalon, E., *Fairy-tale Structures and Motifs in 'Le Grand Meaulnes'* (Frankfurt, Herbert Lang, 1975).

23. Cellier, L., *'Le Grand Meaulnes' ou l'initiation manquée* (Paris, Minard, 1963). Provocative monograph arguing that Meaulnes fails his knightly 'initiation' test.

24. Champigny, R., *Portrait of a Symbolist Hero* (Bloomington, Indiana University Press, 1954). Uneven: some comments are really perceptive, some pretentiously assertive.

25. Giannoni, R., 'Alain-Fournier et Thomas Hardy', *Revue de Littérature Comparée*, 42 (July-Sept. 1968), 407-26. Excellent comparative study.

26. Goldgar, H., 'Alain-Fournier and the initiation archetype', *The French Review*, XLIII, Special issue, No.1 (Winter 1970), 87-99. Examines same question as *22* but answers it more persuasively.

27. Grojnowski, D., 'Le thème de la route dans l'œuvre d'Alain-Fournier', *Critique*, 20 (August-Sept. 1964), 716-29.

28. Gross, R.V., 'The narrator as demon in Grass and Alain-Fournier', *Modern Fiction Studies*, 25 (Winter 1979-80), 625-39. Argues that Seurel's exercise of power is truly demonic.

29. Guiomar, M., *Inconscient et imaginaire dans 'Le Grand Meaulnes'* (Paris, Corti, 1964). Stimulating, very detailed and sometimes over-ingenious thesis that A.-F.'s whole life and work were traumatized by the family's moving house in his early infancy.

30. Locke, F.W., *'Le Grand Meaulnes*: the desire and pursuit of the whole', *Renascence* (Marquette University Press), X (Spring 1959), 135-46.

31. Maclean, M., *Le Jeu suprême: structures et thèmes dans 'Le Grand Meaulnes'* (Paris, Corti, 1973). Structuralist analysis more detailed and much more persuasive than *20*.

32. March, H.M., 'The "other landscape" of Alain-Fournier', *Publications of the Modern Language Association of America*, LVI (1941), 266-79. A comparative essay still worth reading.

33. Schier, D., *'Le Grand Meaulnes'*, *Modern Language Journal*, XXXVI (March 1952), 129-32. The prosecution's case against *Le Grand Meaulnes* pungently presented.

34. Sorrell, M., 'François Seurel's personal adventure in *Le Grand Meaulnes'*, *Modern Language Review*, 69 (1974), 79-87. Seurel redeemed and revenged by his achievement as creative artist.

35. ——, *'Le Grand Meaulnes*: a Bergsonian view of the *fête étrange'*, *Australian Journal of French Studies*, XI (1974), 182-87. Argues that Meaulnes's *domaine* remains *perdu* because events there were enacted in a temporal dimension different from that of the everyday world.

36. Timmermans, G., 'Recherches sur le style poétique du *Grand Meaulnes'*,

Annales de la Faculté de Lettres de Toulouse, 4 (Littératures IV), 5 (1956), 43-89.

37. Turnell, M., 'Alain-Fournier', in *The Rise of the French Novel* (London, Hamish Hamilton, 1979), 221-56. Good general article with some shrewd insights.

38. Ullmann, S., 'The symbol of the sea in *Le Grand Meaulnes*', in *The Image in the Modern French Novel* (Oxford University Press, 1960), 99-123. Perceptive study of Alain-Fournier's use of imagery.

39. Vincenot, C., 'Le rêve dans *Le Grand Meaulnes*', *Revue des Sciences Humaines*, 31 (April-Sept. 1966), 265-96. Detailed and persuasive.

40. Woodcock, G., 'Alain-Fournier and The Lost Land', in *Queen's Quarterly*, 81 (1974), 348-56. Analyses A.-F.'s yearning for his lost childhood vision.

CRITICAL GUIDES TO FRENCH TEXTS

edited by
Roger Little, Wolfgang van Emden, David Williams